THE BULLY PLAYS

24 Short Plays by

Sandra Fenichel Asher
Cherie Bennett
Max Bush
José Casas
Gloria Bond Clunie
Eric Coble
Doug Cooney
Linda Daugherty
Lisa Dillman
Richard Dresser
José Cruz González
Stephen Gregg
D.W. Gregory
Brian Guehring
Dwayne Hartford
Barry Kornhauser
Trish Lindberg
Brett Neveu
Ernie Nolan
R.N. Sandberg
Geraldine Ann Snyder
Werner Trieschmann
Elizabeth Wong
Y York

Compiled and Edited by Linda Habjan
Foreword by Susan Sugerman, MD, MPH

Dramatic Publishing

Woodstock, Illinois • Australia • New Zealand • South Africa

*** NOTICE ***

IMPORTANT BILLING AND CREDIT REQUIREMENTS

All producers of the plays must give credit to the authors of the plays in all programs distributed in connection with performances of the plays and in all instances in which the titles of the plays appear for purposes of advertising, publicizing or otherwise exploiting the plays and/or a production. The names of the authors must also appear on a separate line, on which no other name appears, immediately following the title and must appear in size of type not less than fifty percent (50%) the size of the title type. Biographical information on the authors, if included in the playbook, may be used in all programs. *In all programs this notice must appear:*

"Produced by special arrangement with
THE DRAMATIC PUBLISHING COMPANY of Woodstock, Illinois"

This collection of plays is funny, sad, powerful and important.

Bullying is a catch-phrase for treating others as less than human. All of these plays help teenagers develop their moral imaginations and see that there is no us/them. There is only us.

The Bully Plays *is a tasty antidote to our toxic teen culture.*

– Mary Pipher, Ph.D.

Table of Contents

Foreword

Bullying: Why So Much Drama?

We've all been there. At one time or another, we each have wished someone else would be reasonable and do it our way. We have cajoled, pleaded, begged or pressured another person to understand our own point of view and comply with our wishes. Hopefully, we did this with good intentions and with good reasons. In a perfect world, we want only the best for everyone, if not also for ourselves. But when is the line crossed between kind-hearted persuasion and bullying? Is it always so easy to tell?

Bullying differs from friendly teasing or gentle coaxing. Bullying is aggressive behavior intended to harm or show power over another person that is repeated over time. Teasing can be fun between friends, but it becomes bullying if only one person enjoys it while the other suffers. While taunting is easy to recognize as social aggression, more subtle forms of bullying, such as excluding someone, gossiping or spreading false rumors, can be harder to identify in real time. Bullying also happens when an aggressor tries to get others to join in "disliking" or "disrespecting" someone else, when people use friendship as a weapon for revenge, or when former "friends" withdraw attention to prove a point or display power. Cyberbullying (through the Internet or other electronic media) can include posting photos or comments designed to offend, threaten, harass, or make someone look bad.

Bullies have a strong need to show their dominance over others or to get their own way. While many are well-connected to their peers and have a definite social "power," they may be overly concerned about their popularity. Interestingly, girls are as equally aggressive as boys but tend to use different tactics. Surprisingly, most bullies have average or better-than-average self-esteem; they do not tend to be anxious or insecure. On the other hand, some bullies suffer from depression or anxiety as well as low self-esteem. These children seem to be easily pressured by peers and do not identify with the emotions or feelings of others. Still other risk factors include aggressive behavior, having less parent involvement, impulsive behavior, poor frustration tolerance, and having a positive view of violence. Over the long term, people who bully persistently in childhood never learn realistic long-term friendship skills. They have higher risks of abusing alcohol and other drugs, are more likely to engage in violent and criminal behavior, and are more likely to be abusive toward their romantic partners, spouses or children when they become adults.

Victims of bullying tend to be children who are less popular or new to a situation. Kids who appear anxious or fearful may be easy targets for bullies looking to show themselves as more powerful or intimidating. Children and teens with academic, physical, or social "differences" can experience subtle to severe teasing, taunting and outright abuse, as those in "power" try to assert dominance. Victims tend not to get along well with others, have few friends, and have low self-esteem. Children or teens who do not conform to gender norms may be particularly at risk. Ultimately, kids who get bullied may become secretive, moody, depressed, angry, or may turn to destructive coping behaviors (school avoidance, eating disorders, drug use, self-harm or suicide).

At the extremes, they are more likely to retaliate through extremely violent means.

Bystanders, who don't know what to do, feel powerless and frustrated and may begin to internalize negative feelings for the victim as a way to justify their lack of action. They, too, are at increased risk for alcohol and drug abuse, depression and anxiety, and problems with school attendance or performance. While not directly involved in a bullying situation, during a time when children are supposed to be learning about friendships and intimacy, exposure to bullying can affect everyone's long-term relationship skills.

We know that bullying affects millions of teens every year. It happens in schools, on playgrounds, at summer camps, on the soccer field, and in chess clubs. It happens when adults have their backs turned and even when adults stand in plain view but fail to recognize it or intercede. It happens among peers and between siblings (and even parents). While the basic nature of social aggression in our time may not be so different from what happened a generation or two ago, the changing landscape of our society (e.g. fragmentation of families, increased work and financial demands on parents, let alone technological changes such as the Internet and social media) allows bullying to happen more often, more instantaneously, and more aggressively without the traditional checks and balances of a bygone era.

Why Dramatize Bullying?

While bullying may be pervasive, that doesn't mean it is healthy or normal. True, there is some value in learning to stand up for yourself against those out to humiliate or control you. Learning to bounce back and defend yourself against social aggression builds true and lasting resilience. But it is a mistake to presume that bullying is an expected part of childhood to be tolerated as a "growing pain." We live in a society, unfortunately, where bullying often crosses the line to cause real and lasting pain, dysfunction, and even life-threatening danger. It is time to do something about it.

Within this anthology you will find plays written for youth audiences to be staged by teen actors. As a teenager or an adult involved in these performances, ten minutes spent with any of these stories may change your perspective, open your eyes, or inspire you to do something to help yourself or someone you care about. If experiencing these plays helps even one person to recognize bullying, understand why it is happening, and take steps to stop it, then the effort will have been worth it. When art can be used to improve, not just imitate, life, we are all better off.

Susan Sugerman, MD, MPH
Adolescent Medicine Physician
President and Co-founder of
Girls to Women Health and Wellness
Dallas, Texas

Preface

This anthology was commissioned to provide a format for confronting the issue of bullying and the traumatic, lifelong and sometimes tragic results. Many young people are under siege and fighting to survive in an environment where they feel they have no support—from their parents, teachers, and sometimes even their friends. Bullying can make going to school or a social event an agonizing experience, and it can have long-term adverse effects.

One way to approach such a universal problem is to get it out into the open and provide young people with strategies to deal with it in creative and empowering ways. This anthology of 10-minute plays offers a wide range of perspectives on the subject of bullying from some amazingly insightful and gifted playwrights. The plays themselves are touching, imaginative, powerful, uplifting and often very funny.

The Bully Plays includes 24 10-minute plays by 24 top playwrights. We requested that these authors pursue any and all avenues through which to address the subject and received a wide range of perspectives. These plays focus on bullying as it occurs between and among young people, their parents and siblings. They address the subject from the perspectives of bullies, the bullied and bystanders and revolve around gender, sexuality, physical condition, social status and many other issues. The plays also address how technology has increased not only the methods but also the scope of bullying.

These plays can be performed in any number and combination. You can perform them in traditional settings, such as the classroom or stage, or you can take them to non-traditional venues such as the school cafeteria or even the shopping mall. You can take them on the road to local elementary schools or to youth groups or camps. Because the subject of bullying is often too humiliating and painful to talk about, we hope these plays will stimulate discussion and become part of an ongoing project that will help people deal with bullying in a positive way. They can provide examples of ways to work out differences with respect, compassion, understanding and kindness. They can also help people come up with real solutions and effective ways to break the cycle of bullying. Positive emotions and behaviors are contagious, and this anthology of plays can help you take the steps to reverse the trend of bullying and create a "no tolerance" policy for bullying in your school or community.

Linda Habjan

Alex
(a conversation about nothing)

By José Casas

CHARACTER(S)

ALEX .... an animated 13-year-old boy who likes talking
with his hands and who is on the verge of becoming
a freshman and hiding the pain of being a teenager

SETTING AND TIME: The setting is anyplace a son could
have a conversation with his dad. A chair and television are
located onstage. The time is sometime in the afternoon on
the same day that Alex's school was locked down over an
incident of violence.

WORDS TO PONDER: *"Sticks and stones may break my
bones, but words will never hurt me, but I know that
expression doesn't work."*
– Alex Guillen (my nephew)

*(LIGHTS are dark. The SOUNDS of kids making a
commotion can be heard. An incident of violence is
occurring at a middle school, and kids are reacting to it
from the vantage point of their classrooms. In a sad way,
it should almost sound like the audience cheering the
Roman gladiators in battle. After a few moments,
LIGHTS go up and we see ALEX. It seems like he is
looking out the window. He begins pointing and is in mid-
conversation.)*

1

ALEX *(animated)*. Like I was saying…they put the entire school on lockdown!!! The third time this year… Crazy… We saw the entire scene from class. Jerome went all Grand Theft Auto and everything. You could totally tell he was on drugs or something. Some of the kids say he was on cocaine and others were saying speed. I don't know. I just hear things but, like I was saying…it was, uhm… He looked like he was possessed. He ran away from his P.E. class and was still holding the bat they were using for the softball game. He runs up to Miss Walter's car and begins smashing out the side windows. Coach Liam and the security officer were trying to stop him, but they couldn't get close because he was swinging all over the place. He finally jumps onto the hood of the Prius and starts hitting the windshield. He was destroying that thing and you could tell he was getting angrier and angrier, like he didn't have any control over what he was doing… And everybody in class is crowding the windows to see what's happening even though Mrs. Garcia had told us to stay in our seats. *(Beat; guilty.)* And…I didn't listen to her, but, I should've… I didn't need to see Jerome like that.

(Extended beat. ALEX gets lost in his thoughts. He "snaps" back when a question is posed.)

ALEX *(cont'd)*. Well… He continues doing what he's doing and he hits the windshield a couple more times before he slips and falls. They jump all over him and he's yelling louder and louder and he screams, "I hate them… All of them! It's not fair! It's not my fault!!!" *(Beat; reflecting.)* It was sad. The police cars drove up and Jerome was sitting on the curb with his head in his hands and he kept crying and crying… Not loud crying. Soft crying. All the adults were standing around, but none of them were talking to him. Not one word... Nothing. *(Beat; sympathetic.)* He looked all alone.

(Extended beat. ALEX responds to a question.)

ALEX *(cont'd)*. My friend Liz said that kids on the other team were talking trash. They were always making fun of him... Always making his life miserable. I'm surprised he didn't go crazier sooner... You would've thought he would have bullied them... You see, Jerome is a big guy... Really big... I don't understand why anyone would want to pick on him. He's like already six feet tall and over two hundred pounds and he's older than all of the kids in school because he was held back a couple of times... Made people think he was stupid... He reminded me of this character named Lenny in that book *Of Mice and Men*. You ever read it? *(Beat; responding.)* I didn't really talk to him. I mean, I didn't have anything against him. I'd say "hi" to him in the mornings or "bye" to him when school let out... But, he kept to himself... He didn't have any friends... Not sure he wanted any.

(Extended beat. ALEX responds to a question.)

ALEX *(cont'd)*. Yeah... I felt sorry for him. Nobody deserves to be treated that way. One time... *(Beat.)* One time they even cornered him in the locker room and held him on the ground and they ripped his shirt. They kept punching and squeezing him, like...

(ALEX pauses, then mimics breasts being squeezed; embarrassed.)

ALEX *(cont'd)*. You know... They said he had boobs... Like a girl.

(Extended beat. ALEX responds to a question.)

ALEX *(cont'd)*. Yeah...we have a lot of them at school. They think they're all that and they act like they own the place... Always talking like in the movies. *(Demonstrating.)* "Yo, homie. You best be giving me my respect." Ignorant stuff like that. They want to act all gangster. They mess with the kids who aren't as popular as they are and they punk them in different ways. They're always menacing them if they don't do certain things they want and they'll have their friends jump them... But they always get away with it. Even with the security guys walking around... And, the teachers try and help, but they do the stuff when the teachers aren't looking, and by the time the teachers come back, well... The damage has already been done. *(Beat; annoyed.)* These bullies play with their heads more than anything else. I think that's worse, and the older kids...they punk on smaller kids that can't defend themselves. It's easy pickings... But it's the worst for kids like Jerome; the ones who have weight problems. If someone walks in from another classroom and if they're a little chunky you could hear kids cracking jokes. Kids will whisper and point and start laughing. It usually starts off with fat jokes like "you so fat, your blood type is maple syrup" or something lame like that... But it doesn't take long before it gets really vicious to the point where kids can't take it anymore. *(Beat.)* The worst thing to be in our school is...fat. If you're fat, you're the first target... The biggest target.

(Extended beat. ALEX sits down and fidgets in his seat.)

ALEX *(cont'd)*. Sometimes they mess with kids with the race thing, too. You hear the N-word all the time... Or they'll pick on you if you're Mexican. *(Beat.)* They make fun of Marshall because he lives in a trailer park. They're always calling him a redneck or trailer trash and they make fun of his clothes... But you know what? Marshall's going to get the last laugh. You know how smart he is. He's going to be the successful one, not them. *(Beat; seething.)* I get sick of them... The Mess With Me types. They're like, "If you mess with me, I'll mess with you," but no one ever messes with them. That's the point. They always start it... But nothing is done about it; at least, not to them. The ones who get busted are usually the kids who fight back. They get caught throwing punches. It's the innocent kids who get suspended... The ones who get expelled.

(Extended beat. ALEX points at the television set.)

ALEX *(cont'd)*. I hear about bullying on the news all the time. You hear stories about kids being bullied because they're gay, or they show stuff about sexting and how it spreads so fast and so quickl—

(ALEX is interrupted. Beat; responding, annoyed.)

ALEX *(cont'd)*. Yeah, yeah, yeah... I'm not a little kid anymore, I know what it is. *(Beat.)* But, sometimes the bullying from *(air quotes)* "the females" is even worse... Like *Girls Gone Wild*... They like to spread rumors like wildfire. For example, there was this one girl at my school who was pregnant already, but she had a miscarriage or something. They always gossiped about her and spread these terrible lies about her and her family...

They said it was her fault that the baby died. How jacked-up is that? *(Beat; irked.)* It's like they don't have anything better to do... I even heard about this one story on the *Oprah Show* about how this one girl's mom was messing with another girl that her daughter was fighting with... She went cyber-bully on her all over the Internet. She was texting this other girl and pretending to be a cute boy, so the girl falls in love with the boy who doesn't even exist. The mom stops texting the other girl, and the other girl gets so sad that she kills herself? *(Beat; confused.)* Why would a mother do that? She's supposed to be the adult.

(Extended beat.)

ALEX *(cont'd).* It makes me not want to watch TV anymore. It's so depressing. *(Beat.)* It's like these jerks really-really-really want to hurt you, so when it gets to that point you need to talk to someone...or just walk away, it's not worth it anymore...it's frustrating when kids don't get help because you want to get involved... But it's not really your place to because... *(Beat.)* It's not like my battle to fight for them. *(Beat; standing up.)* People who bully people want to see you cry. I think they've been bullied. I think they struggle at home with their own problems. They feel like if they harass somebody else, that will make them feel better about themselves... Then, you have those bullies who cause drama just for the fun of it... They just have no heart. *(Beat.)* That's why I like *Bully Beatdown*. Have you seen it? *(Beat; excited.)* Oh, man... You have to step into the twenty-first century... You don't know what you're missing... It's the best show on MTV!

(ALEX begins to mimic an MMA fighter move.)

ALEX *(cont'd).* I love Mayhem. He's the host... He's this professional MMA fighter, so you can tell he can be a bully if he wanted to, but he doesn't. He's nice and he's funny and he helps the people who can't defend themselves. *(Amused.)* The bullies try to act all hard like it's not a big deal. They talk and talk about what they're going to do against their opponents in the cage, but it only takes them a couple of seconds before they realize they're dead meat... I love seeing the bullies when they get beat up. I like how the bully gets what he deserves... And sometimes the bullies still stay bullies. They don't learn anything...even after getting their butts kicked. *(Beat; content.)* For me, though...the best part is when a bully shakes hands with his victims. You can see it on their faces. They know they were wrong... I like that it's not really revenge. It's just them being taught a lesson... That's all.

(Extended beat. ALEX responds to a question.)

ALEX *(cont'd).* I don't know.

(Extended beat.)

ALEX *(cont'd).* No... Not really... I don't see it getting any better. *(Beat; pessimistic.)* It's not right... Kids hurting other kids... Because it hurts them inside and it messes them up for the course of their lives... People forget that kids who get bullied become adults... Adults who never grow up from that... They still have that scar in their lives. I don't get it... Why bother messing with people who never did anything to you? Why bully someone else when you can live a good life? *(Beat; pensive.)* You know…I always hear people say "sticks and stones may break my bones but words will never hurt me." *(Beat; defeated.)* But…I know that expression doesn't work.

(Extended beat. ALEX hears a question but doesn't respond; beat. He looks down to the ground.)

ALEX *(cont'd)*. Me?

(Extended beat.)

ALEX *(cont'd, quietly)*. I don't want to talk about it, Dad.

(Extended beat.)

ALEX *(cont'd, sadly whispering)*. It's…nothing.

END OF PLAY

Beasts

By Ernie Nolan

CHARACTERS

SETTING AND TIME: An elaborate and foreboding labyrinth in ancient Greece.

(DARKNESS. The air is sticky and foggy. Offstage, the voice of a young man is heard echoing through the chambers of a labyrinth.)

THESEUS *(offstage)*. Beast? Beast come out from hiding!

(THESEUS, a small young man, tentatively enters, holding a ball of gold string, which continues offstage, and an enormous sword.)

THESEUS *(cont'd)*. I know you're somewhere near, beast!

(A SOUND, which sounds like a howl and a yawn, is heard. THESEUS jumps.)

THESEUS *(cont'd)*. Show yourself!

(The yawn/howl SOUND is heard again. THESEUS readies his sword.)

THESEUS *(cont'd)*. If you know what's good for you. I won't ask for you to appear again.

(The SOUND of giant hooves on stone comes nearer and nearer. THESEUS swallows and tries to stand bravely. Enter ASTERION, a Minotaur. There is a silent stare-down between the two, and then...)

THESEUS *(cont'd)*. Beast, prepare to cross the river Styx, 'cause Hades awaits! *(He lifts his giant sword. Beat.)*
ASTERION. You have got to be kidding me. I woke up from a nap for this?

(ASTERION turns and exits. THESEUS stands there, dumbfounded.)

THESEUS. Beast?... Beast?... Where are you going?
ASTERION *(offstage)*. Anywhere I don't have to deal with you.
THESEUS. But...but you... You have to return!
ASTERION. Why?
THESEUS. Because I command you to!
ASTERION. You what?
THESEUS. I'm a prince, and you have to do what I say.
ASTERION. Says who?
THESEUS. My dad.

ASTERION. He can jump into the sea for all I care!

THESEUS. Can't you come out here so we can settle this like men?

ASTERION. Men? I'm half bull and you're a boy.

THESEUS. Am not!

ASTERION. Are too!

THESEUS. Am not!

ASTERION. Are too!

THESEUS. OK...you might have a point. I am on the young-ish side.

ASTERION. "Ish"? I know goats older than you.

THESEUS. Can't you just...

ASTERION. No! Go away! I'm done dealing with you, runt!

THESEUS. But...

ASTERION. Head back to whatever acropolis you came from...

THESEUS. But...

ASTERION. What? Is this all Greek to you? Goooooooo-oooo!

(The SOUND of ASTERION's "Goooo!" echoes through the chamber. THESEUS stands, confused; he definitely planned this to go differently. He tries to fight back tears, but alas, they get the better of him. He drops his sword, falls to his knees and begins to cry. A moment later, we hear from offstage...)

ASTERION *(cont'd).* Little annoying intruder? *(THESEUS cries more.)* Little annoying intruder, are you OK? *(THESEUS cries even more.)* Did you fall or something? *(He enters.)* Hey...you all right?

THESEUS. Do I look all right?

ASTERION. I don't know. Maybe emotional meltdowns are the norm for you.

THESEUS. Well, they aren't. I've been under a lot of stress lately.

ASTERION. Oh yeah?

THESEUS. Yeah. See…growing up in Troezen, I didn't know who my dad was, and recently I moved this rock and I found this sword, a really uncomfortable pair of shoes, and my dad's name underneath it…and I found out my dad was the King of Athens. So I took this really long trip to Athens to meet him and had to fight all of these wicked bandits, only to discover that my stepmother was crazy… Seriously! She tried to poison me…and then, basically, he gave me this challenge and I know that if I do it, it will really impress him, and then I know he'll like being my dad.

ASTERION. Really? What's the challenge?

THESEUS. I have to destroy you. *(Beat.)*

ASTERION. For real? *(Beat.)*

THESEUS. Yep. I have to destroy you and then sail a white flag on the boat when I return.

ASTERION. That's kinda weird.

THESEUS. I know, but that's what he told me to do.

ASTERION. I don't get it, though.

THESEUS. I think it has something to do with being able to see the white from a far distance…

ASTERION. Not the flag…destroying me. Why are people always trying to destroy me? I don't get it. This has been going on for a while now.

THESEUS. Well…

ASTERION. If you have insights, I would love to hear them.

THESEUS. Well... I mean...look at you...the things you do...the way you've treated people...well, you're like you said: half man and half beast...you're different.

ASTERION. I'm different?

THESEUS. Yes. You're different.

ASTERION. "You're different," says the crying boy holding a ball of yarn.

THESEUS. It's not yarn. It's a ball of thread. This girl gave it to me to chart my way down here. She called it a momonic device.

ASTERION. I think you mean mnemonic device.

THESEUS. Same thing

ASTERION. No it isn't. It's "mnemonic" not "momonic." I happen to know the goddess of memory personally, and her name is Mnemosyne not Momosyne.

THESEUS. Well, aren't you special!

ASTERION. Yes, I am!

THESEUS. Ah ha!

ASTERION. Ah ha, what?

THESEUS. So if you're special, then you're different!

ASTERION. If you're thinking different from *you*, then most certainly...

THESEUS. Yes!

ASTERION. But not different for where I come from.

THESEUS. Listen, your mommy may tell you...

ASTERION. Hey, let's keep my mother out of this. She's got some issues. OK?

THESEUS. OK. Fair enough, beast.

ASTERION. Can I ask you something?

THESEUS. I think that's only fair, before I attempt to destroy you.

ASTERION. Why do you keep on using that word?

THESEUS. Which word? "Destroy"? I don't know...poetic effect maybe.

ASTERION. Not that word. "Beast." How are you using that word?

THESEUS. What do you mean?

ASTERION. Well, are you using that word in order to call me a person who is exceptionally good at something, like, "Man, that Olympian is a beast!"

THESEUS. No. Definitely not. More in the sense of any mammal other than a human...lower than a human...sub-human...like a pig. No...more like a shrimp.

ASTERION. A shrimp?

THESEUS. Yeah. Like something with a disposable head.

ASTERION. A shrimp is not a mammal.

THESEUS. Well, OK...animal then. An animal other than human.

ASTERION. But I'm part human.

THESEUS. Yeah, but only part. You already said you were part cow.

ASTERION. Bull.

THESEUS *(thinking he disagreed)*. No, you did.

ASTERION. Bull.

THESEUS. You did! I wish a scribe would have been here to write it down.

ASTERION. I know I said something, but I didn't say "cow." I'm part bull.

THESEUS. Well, whatever. You can't tell me you know anyone else in the world like you.

ASTERION. What does that matter?

THESEUS. Well, you're not like everyone else and between that and some of the things you've done...my dad wants you destroyed...in fact, I think *your* dad wants you destroyed, too.

ASTERION. That's a terrible assumption.

THESEUS. Well, it's the truth! Why else would he put you in this underground maze?

ASTERION. It's the foundation for condos! He's building me condos, OK?

THESEUS. Give me a break! He thinks that you're an ugly, hideous, monstrous freak and he wants to hide you away because you're different from everyone else.

ASTERION. Oh, really? *(Calling offstage.)* Hey, Yannis…

YANNIS *(offstage)*. Yeah?

ASTERION. You got a sec? Can you come out here?

YANNIS. Yeah, sure thing, "Cous."

ASTERION *(to THESEUS)*. Let's see who's different, shall we?

(Enter YANNIS, another Minotaur.)

YANNIS. Whassup?

ASTERION *(referencing THESEUS)*. Check that out.

YANNIS. Who's he?

ASTERION. The "man" who's going to destroy me, apparently.

YANNIS. Destroy you? Why?

ASTERION. 'Cause I'm different, according to his dad. Apparently, my dad thinks so too, so he wants me gone as well.

YANNIS. Uncle Minos? You gotta be kidding!

ASTERION. Nope. Just ask him.

(YANNIS crosses to get in THESEUS' face.)

YANNIS. What's your problem, little dude?

THESEUS *(trying to be strong)*. My name's not Little Dude. It's Theseus.

YANNIS. That's a big name for such a little dude.

ASTERION. How about we call him Lil' T?

YANNIS *(turning to ASTERION)*. I like the sound of that.
That's good! *(Back to THESEUS.)* What's your deal, Lil'
T? Why you causing problems with that ball of yarn?

THESEUS. It's not a ball of yarn! It's thread. It's my
bubonnic device.

ASTERION. Mnemonic.

THESEUS. Who cares?

YANNIS. I'll tell you what I care about…why are you all
up here in our labyrinth?

THESEUS. I… Ummmm…well…

YANNIS. What's with the freezing up? I ain't Medusa!

ASTERION. Told ya, "Cous." He wants me gone, 'cause
I'm different.

YANNIS. Well, that's very funny to me, 'cause right now
he's the one that's different.

THESEUS. But there are only two of you!

ASTERION. Here, right now. Yes.

THESEUS. Are you trying to tell me there are more freaky
beasts like you? Please! You're oddities! Ugly oddities
that are all on your own!

ASTERION *(calling offstage)*. Yo, Antonia.

ANTONIA *(offstage)*. Yeah?

ASTERION. You doin' anything?

ANTONIA. About to paint my hooves…why?

ASTERION. Could you come out here for a sec?

ANTONIA. Sure…hold on.

THESEUS. Who's that?

YANNIS. You'll see, Lil' T.

(Enter ANTONIA, a female Minotaur.)

ANTONIA. There a problem?

YANNIS *(pointing at THESEUS)*. A little one standing right
there.

ANTONIA. Who's that?

ASTERION. Lil' T. He's come to destroy me.

ANTONIA. He gonnna do that with that ball of yarn?

THESEUS. It's not a ball of yarn! It's thread! Haven't you ever seen a ball of thread before? This really hot girl handed it to me before I came down here and…

ANTONIA. So you could do what? Knit a tunic?

THESEUS. No! So I could remember the way back. This string is tied to the entrance of this place. I'll just follow it back when I'm done. It's like a poponic device.

ASTERION. Mnemonic device.

THESEUS. Whatever! It's not about the device. It's not about the thread. It's not about any of those things. I don't care about those things!

ANTONIA. It doesn't look that way.

YANNIS. You look quite upset.

THESEUS. I wish you all would just leave me alone! *(He breaks down and begins to cry again.)*

ANTONIA. What's his deal?

ASTERION. I don't know. He just does that. He just breaks into tears.

YANNIS. Listen, kid. I'm sorry you're feeling all bent out of shape and everything, but I don't think we can leave you alone.

THESEUS. Why not?

YANNIS. Because you're here to destroy a member of my family and I got a problem with that!

ANTONIA. Me too!

YANNIS. You think you're all cool, struttin' in here with your big sword and your ball of yarn…

THESEUS *(through tears)*. It's thread.

YANNIS. But destroying my cousin just 'cause he's different…

THESEUS. He's also pillaged and plundered villages…

ASTERION. OK, maybe a few here and there…

THESEUS. And eaten whole herds of sheep that weren't his…

ASTERION. But if people are going to just leave them outside like that…

THESEUS. And he's taken innocent lives… *(Beat.)*

ASTERION. So what are you trying to get at?

THESEUS. You've upset and hurt people. You're brutal and uncivilized and filthy…

ANTONIA. We can't invite those centaurs over for dinner anymore. They always mess up the place.

THESEUS. You're a beast…a fiend. Can't you see why people would want you gone?

ASTERION. Well, what about you?

THESEUS. What about me?

ASTERION. You're not perfect.

THESEUS. What are you implying?

ASTERION. I'm not implying. I'm saying. You're not perfect. You've hurt people.

THESEUS. Who?

ASTERION. What about those bandits you mentioned earlier?

THESEUS. They were thugs! They deserved what they got.

ASTERION. Who are you to sit in judgment of what other people deserve?

THESEUS. I'm a prince.

YANNIS. That doesn't make you any better than us.

THESEUS. Well, people think I'm a hero. *(The MINO-TAURS laugh.)* Well, it may not look like it to you, but I'm gonna go down in history for what I've done some day.

ANTONIA. I'm tired of listening to this pipsqueak's yammering.

YANNIS. He's triggering a migraine. What do you say to silencing him for good, "Cous"?

ASTERION. Well, if today is Destroy-the-Thing-That's-Different Day, who are we not to partake in the celebration?

YANNIS. I'm feelin' a party up in here. What about you, Antonia?

ANTONIA. Oh, I'm feelin' like partyin' like it's 1999 B.C.E.

ASTERION. Well then… Let's get this party started.

(GEORGE, another young man, runs in, stops between THESEUS and the MINOTAURS.)

GEORGE *(threateningly)*. Back off, beasts!

THESEUS. George! How did you find me?

GEORGE. I followed the yarn tied to the entrance of the maze.

THESEUS. It's thread, not yarn.

GEORGE. Really? At that thickness you could knit a really nice tunic. *(Turning to the MINOTAURS.)* Prepare your wages for Charon, beasts! *(He raises his sword. The MINOTAURS laugh.)* What?

YANNIS. You seriously think that you alone can stop the three of us?

GEORGE. There's also His Highness.

YANNIS. Who? Lil' T?

GEORGE. Lil' T?

THESEUS. I'll explain later.

ANTONIA. You two can't take the three of us.

(Enter another young man, GEORGE II.)

GEORGE II. It would be fairer if it were three on three.

ASTERION. Who are you?

GEORGE II. I'm George's cousin George. *(Huffing and puffing, turning to THESEUS and GEORGE.)* Can we get this over, guys? My asthma is really starting to act up down here. *(Directed at the MINOTAURS.)* Hope your maps are ready for a trip to the underworld, beasts. *(He strikes a menacing pose with his sword.)*

ASTERION. You're both named George?

GEORGE. It's a family name. Kinda like yours, beast.

YANNIS. Them's fighting words, Lil' G.

GEORGE. Lil' G?

THESEUS. They have this nickname thing…just go with it.

GEORGE II *(breathing heavily)*. Guys, I hate to be a buzz kill, but can we just rid the world of beasts and get back up above ground? Between the mold and the animal hair, I'm really having a tough time.

YANNIS. Why's he breathing like that?

GEORGE. That's just what he does sometimes.

YANNIS. Well, how come you two don't do that?

GEORGE. 'Cause he's got asthma. We don't.

YANNIS. So he's different than you two.

THESEUS. Well… I guess…but…

YANNIS. So if he's different, why don't you destroy him?

ANTONIA. Let's destroy all of them! There's a snack for each of us now. We don't have to share.

ASTERION. Funny how things just happen to work out!

(The MINOTAURS begin to walk forward to the BOYS when a YOUNG GIRL, enters with a sword and stops them.)

GEORGIA. Who's ready for a one-way ticket to Hades?

ASTERION. Don't tell me *you're* a cousin who's named George!

GEORGIA. Don't be ridiculous! My name's not George. It's Georgia.

YANNIS. How many more of you are there?

GEORGIA. I'm the only Georgia.

YANNIS. No. In your group.

GEORGE. Fourteen of us traveled to Crete.

GEORGE II. The other nine are outside.

GEORGIA. They're on their way down here, actually. Whoever thought of tying that yarn to the entrance was brilliant!

(The GROUP looks at THESEUS for a response.)

THESEUS. I give up. It's thread…but we'll call it yarn. It's just easier.

GEORGE. You're soon to be outnumbered, beasts!

ASTERION. You know, I'm getting a little ticked off. I don't think I like that word.

GEORGE II. Well, "critter" just doesn't seem an appropriate synonym.

GEORGIA. And "ignoramus" is a mouthful.

THESEUS. What about "troglodyte"?

GEORGE. Nah, that doesn't come trippingly off of the tongue.

THESEUS. Then I guess you're stuck with "beast," beast.

ASTERION. And I think you're stuck with getting your neck wrung, Lil' T.

THESEUS. Bring it, beast!

ASTERION. It's here, twerp!

(It looks like there will be a great altercation. The two GROUPS aggressively step toward each other to fight when POLYPHEMUS, a Cyclops, enters, limping.)

POLYPHEMUS. Excuse me…

(The two factions stop in their tracks and look at the intruder.)

POLYPHEMUS *(cont'd)*. I was in pursuit of this really smokin' sea nymph who ran down here, but I tripped over some random strung-up yarn and she got away. Now I'm totally lost and I think I need medical attention. Could someone tell me how to get out of this place?

THESEUS. What are you?

POLYPHEMUS. Me? A Cyclops. The name's Polyphemus and I'm…

YANNIS. Malformed.

GEORGIA. Grotesque.

ANTONIA. Monstrous.

GEORGE. Misshapen.

GEORGE II. Odd.

THESEUS. Different.

ASTERION. A beast. Do you know, Polyphemus, what happens to beasts?

POLYPHEMUS. What's that?

ASTERION. Shall we show him, Lil' T?

(ASTERION looks at THESEUS, who understands what he is saying. The two then start to walk in POLY-PHEMUS' direction with their groups in tow.)

POLYPHEMUS. Guys, that's nice of you, but everybody doesn't have to walk me out…

(LIGHTS fade out as the GROUPS get closer.)

END OF PLAY

Blu

By Gloria Bond Clunie

CHARACTERS

BLU PETERSON................. an eighth-grader (gender may be
    flexible and pronouns throughout play changed accordingly)
SCOTT ....Blu's brother, high-school junior
MORGAN .... Scott's friend, high-school junior
JUSTIN............................. Scott's friend, high-school junior
DEE .... Scott's friend, high-school junior
MRS. PETERSON .... mother of Blu and Scott

SETTING AND TIME: Blu's bedroom—his world—*or* a
dark space with bright colors. Now.

*(BLU's bedroom. BLU's books, paintings and poems fill
the room. The bed is almost made. It feels as if BLU just
stepped out for a minute. The room can be realistic,
mimed or imagined with cubes, platforms and empty
frames. BLU sits curled in a corner, head down, quietly
rocking. SCOTT enters, followed by MORGAN, JUSTIN
and DEE who look at the paintings in the room. They do
not see BLU, but BLU sees them.)*

MORGAN. Wow!
SCOTT. What?
MORGAN. I just…
SCOTT. This your first time in here?
MORGAN. I just… I never imagined…

JUSTIN. It is kind of…
DEE. Amazing?
BLU. You like it? You really like it?
MORGAN *(points to another painting on the wall)*. That's you! That's you! You look…
SCOTT. Smart?
JUSTIN. Maybe not.
BLU *(looking at painting)*. I wanted to make him look smart. He is smart. He's the smartest big brother you could have. 'Specially if you've only got one. He looks…
SCOTT. Awesome?
MORGAN. Well…kind of incredible. I mean, for you. He made you look…
SCOTT. Well, it's not like he started with dog poop.
MORGAN. But the light. The way he's got the light on your face. Makes you look… Sophomore year, my art teacher tried to show me. I never got it. And I'm good. Real good. But I can never quite get it, the light, to shine through like that, just so. It's like a freaking Rembrandt.

(JUSTIN examines another picture. ALL study it.)

DEE. Is that Ms. Rainer? Dag! Looks just like her.
JUSTIN. Yeah, that funny way her eyes bug out when you do some-thing good.
DEE. Got it down cold. The way she opens her mouth— wide like—and says, "Ohhhhhhhhhhh!"
BLU. And holds it forever!
DEE & BLU. "Ohhhhhhhhhhhhhh!"
DEE. Then breaks out laughing!
BLU. Love her laugh.
SCOTT. Yeah. He really liked her. Said she was the only one that…didn't have to use words. She got it. Got him.

MORGAN *(looking at another painting)*. God, how old was he when he did this one?

BLU. Nine!

DEE *(reading title under painting)*. "Lupicious Lion, Mom and Me." The colors are so bright!

BLU. That day the zoo was mine! All mine. It was right after... Well. We spent the whole day there. Mom and me. And we had popcorn. Smelled so good. We had popcorn and hotdogs and... And we gave all the animals names. Crazy names. Like Lupicious Delgado Lion. And Effie the Effervescent Elephant. You should have seen Gregory the Gorgeous Giraffe! You missed it, Scott. You were in school, or somewhere with Dad. And it was just me and Mom. We sat by the swan lake and watched them sail, sail away, like white-feathered ships out to sea. And Mom. Sitting there, the sun on her face, she was so pretty, sun so pretty in her hair. That night—couldn't get the animals out of my head. Angling their necks, staring into my eyes, like they were trying to tell me something. Like, maybe, they wanted me to set them free, but I didn't know how. The sun, and Mom and Lupicious Delgado Lion! I wanted to hold on to that day forever.

SCOTT. Mom caught him. Three o'clock in the morning, painting away. He was weird like that. An idea would pop into his head, and he'd be up all hours of the night, painting, or writing, or singing. He would wake up singing at the top of his lungs in the middle of the night! Said a song just came to him.

BLU. My head was so full. It would just start racing. So much to think about.

JUSTIN *(reading the title under the picture)*. What kind of kid comes up with a name like Lupicious? Lupicious Lion. I always thought he was a weird kind of little kid. I mean no offense, but... He sure could draw. Your mom, she looks—happy there.

SCOTT. Yeah.

DEE. Is that—Blu?

SCOTT. He painted it, last month, I think. Called it...

BLU. "My Picasso Me."

MORGAN. The colors seem—well, not as intense. *(Studying pictures and poems on the wall.)*

JUSTIN. Who knew? I mean, he always seemed like this geeky little kid. No offense, but Katrina was always talking about how weird he was in class.

MORGAN. Like your sister knows from weird.

JUSTIN. But he wore those crazy clothes.

SCOTT. He liked color.

BLU. Like a rainbow! I'll share my colors. If you let me, I can show you how to strut them!

JUSTIN. I get it, now. I mean, *(looks around room)* I get it now! But when the whole class is in blue jeans and a T-shirt, and you're...

(JUSTIN holds up a colorful shirt. BLU snatches up another one.)

BLU. *Fearless!*

MORGAN. Brave enough to be different!

JUSTIN. Or stupid enough.

MORGAN. Justin!

JUSTIN. Sorry.

SCOTT. I know. We all are.

MOM *(offstage)*. Scott? Scott? Have you found it?

SCOTT *(shouting to his mom offstage)*. Still looking!

MOM. You want help?

SCOTT *(shouting to his mom offstage)*. We got it! *(To MORGAN, JUSTIN and DEE.)* Come on. We have to find it before she comes up here. All she does is cry when she comes up here.

JUSTIN. So it looks like…?

SCOTT. It's blue.

MORGAN. Of course.

SCOTT. About this big. He carried it around, all the time. Wouldn't go anyplace without it. Always writing in it. Big rubber band, holding it together.

DEE. Any idea where it is?

SCOTT. My brother is a pack rat. A neat pat rat, but a pack rat. Why don't you take those drawers over there? Morgan, give me a hand with the closet.

(JUSTIN starts going through the drawers. MORGAN begins in the closet.)

SCOTT *(cont'd)*. And Dee, be my guest! *(He points under the bed.)* We call it…

BLU & SCOTT. The Cove!

BLU. A place of secret treasure!

SCOTT. When he was really tiny, he would have these nightmares. Scared to death of this green-eyed monster under his bed. One night I climbed in beside him and told him all about…

BLU & SCOTT. Ye Good Ole Pirate Pete!

SCOTT. And how good ole Pete the Pirate needed a safe place to stash his treasure.

BLU & SCOTT *(very dramatically)*. He'd steal from the rich and give to the poor!

MORGAN. Sounds like Robin Hood to me.

SCOTT. Hey, he was only five. So we agreed, Pete could stash his treasure in The Cove. Now, Pete was a really good guy, but he was still a pirate, and a swordsman who could swash and buckle with the best of them, and he was not about to let any green-eyed monster mess with his treasure.

DEE. No more green-eyed monster?

SCOTT. Right! Then one day, Blu told me he talked to Pete.

BLU. I did.

SCOTT. Asked him if he could store some of *his own* treasure in The Cove. For safekeeping, you know. Said, kids at school were always taking his stuff. Lunch, and pencils, and his sweat shirt—that was all right, but…

BLU. There was some stuff I had to keep safe. Some of me, I had to keep safe.

SCOTT. And according to Blu, Pete said, "Sure, matey." Soooo… *Voilà!*

(SCOTT pulls a large box, painted like a treasure chest, from underneath the bed.)

BLU. Careful!

SCOTT. Secret treasure.

(As DEE searches through the box, MORGAN pulls out a cape from the closet.)

MORGAN. Look! It's like Joseph's Coat of Many Colors.

SCOTT. He made it himself. One Halloween. Had saved up all these bits of fabric. Sewed it on this old black cape Mom had, and suddenly it was—miraculous.

BLU. You can put it on.

MORGAN. Do you think he'd mind?

BLU. Go ahead. Put it on. I loved wearing it. Put it on. I loved wearing it until…

SCOTT. It's okay.

BLU & SCOTT. "I bring you rainbows!"

SCOTT. He would say that sometimes.

BLU & SCOTT. "I bring you rainbows!"

SCOTT. Might have been his first words. He'd get all excited about this color, or that color, and he'd gather stuff up, stuff with color in it, like he...like he needed it.

BLU. Why live in such a gray world!?!

SCOTT. Could be cloth, or balls, or pieces of paper...string. Would gather it up, come racing at you ninety million miles an hour, tripping all over himself, shouting—

BLU. "I bring you rainbows! See! Can't you *see* the rainbows?"

SCOTT. Inside, he was just like that cape.

BLU. If you could only see the rainbows!

SCOTT. When things got bad, really bad, he'd come home, and sit in that corner and wrap up in it. Said it made him invisible. Said no one could see him in it. That all you could see was color, beautiful color, and he was invisible. That no one ever really saw him anyway, so he might as well be invisible. He took it to school that last week. They had to write a poem in reading class. Write it, then read it to the class the next day. He didn't just want to read his. He wanted to "present it"!

JUSTIN. Katrina said it was really good.

SCOTT. Mom read it, too. Said it would be perfect, tomorrow, at the... Thinks he would like it, if we read it tomorrow. But he didn't turn it in, and we couldn't find a copy in his locker. It must be in his journal. He put everything he loved in there. That day he read it in class? Seemed everybody liked it. Liked it when he finished, then twirled around and around in his cape.

JUSTIN. Katrina said, "It was like he was making his own breeze! Floating on air!"

SCOTT. Then some jerk called him "Gay"! Knocked the wind out of his sails. And before lunch, when he was putting the cape back in his locker, Malik grabbed it, and this dumb bunch of eighth-graders tossed it back and forth, shouting "fag" and...

JUSTIN. Katrina said when Mr. Davis made them give it back, Blu wrapped up in it and started whispering, "You can't see me! You can't touch me! I'm not here." Said it was kind of scary. Him crying and all, standing in the locker room, in this cape. Said it was a really pretty cape.

SCOTT. I wish I could've been there. Could have swashed, and buckled, and cut them down to size, the hateful bastards. *[Note: or dogs.]* If only I had been there.

JUSTIN. You didn't...

SCOTT. What? Say it. Why won't anybody say it? Say it! Hang him? I didn't hang him. We didn't hang him!

MORGAN. Nobody put a rope around his neck. He... He did that.

BLU. I was so lonely...

SCOTT *(talks to the picture on the wall)*. Slipping through the cracks. I didn't see you...

BLU. Nobody sees. Nobody notices.

SCOTT. How could I catch you when I didn't see you falling?

BLU. All you had to do was look!

JUSTIN. It wasn't your fault.

BLU. I was getting all gray inside. Everywhere, except here with my colors, was gray. But you wouldn't let me stay, would you? Mom, Dad, you. Said I had to go to school. For what? So they could *accidentally* knock my lunch in my lap, then laugh? Put shit *[Note: or pee]* in my locker? Hide my books? Call me...

SCOTT. They couldn't keep pulling you out of school! You can't spend your life at the zoo!

BLU. I lived in the zoo! *(Rushes to the picture of "Lupicious Lion.")* I need to go back! Set the animals free!

SCOTT. Grow up! Suck it up! Stop being so damned weird!

(Beat.)

BLU. Nobody sees the colors I see.
SCOTT. Nobody looks.
JUSTIN. You can't blame…
SCOTT. Words we said, and didn't say. Every "Be a big
     boy!" when some stupid kid made him feel small. We
     went on living our lives, when he was living hell. Year
     after year, and he still painted pictures until…
BLU. I just couldn't find the colors anymore. *(Points to his
     heart.)* It was so gray. They made my life so gray.
DEE *(takes a blue notebook out of the Treasure Box)*. Is this
     it?
BLU. Careful.

*(SCOTT takes the journal, turns pages, stops near the
end.)*

SCOTT. It's here. *(He reads from the journal.)* "I don't
     know…"

(ALL look at the journal as BLU "presents" his poem.)

BLU.
     "I don't know how to be among you,
          in a world of limited color.
     Don't know what to do or say,
     I don't understand gray.

     Red, yellow, green, blue
     So many hues to choose!

     Could wear jeans, just like you,
     Comb my hair, just like you,

Get a shirt, just like you
Red-yellow-green, but then I wouldn't be Blu.

(BLU puts on the cape and twirls around.)

So many different shades!
Imagine mine!

'Cause you just see my outline.
I'd draw a picture,
But I'm afraid you might still not see,
All the shades that make up me.

So I fold my paper,
Tuck it away,
Hoping you'll ask
"What's that?" one day.

"What's that?"
And I'll say,
"Color! Technicolor Rainbows! That's me."

(MRS. PETERSON comes to the door. She hesitates, then cautiously enters the room.)

MRS. PETERSON. Did you find it?

(SCOTT hands his mother the journal. MRS. PETERSON turns to exit, then turns back.)

MRS. PETERSON *(cont'd)*. And a tie? He'll need a tie.
SCOTT. Which one?

(SCOTT holds up a blue tie and a rainbow-colored tie for his mother.)

MRS. PETERSON. Blue… *(She takes the blue tie.)* One day he asked me…
BLU. Why am I named Blu?

MRS. PETERSON.
I was laying in the grass looking up at the sky,
wishing for something wonderful, a miracle!
I watched the clouds dance,
and the different shades of heaven roll by,
was wishing for a miracle,
and that miracle was you!
So I called you…I called you—Blu.

SCOTT. He was like the sky, only nobody looked up.

(MRS. PETERSON looks at the tie in her hands.)

MRS. PETERSON. Blue, or maybe… *(She takes the rainbow tie.)*

(ALL exit, except BLU. BLU wraps himself in the cape, twirls around, then slowly takes the cape off.)

BLU. Technicolor Rainbows! That's me!

(LIGHTS fade out.)

END OF PLAY

Bully-Bully

By Cherie Bennett

CHARACTERS

J'NEECE .... age 14, a cheerleader, newest and youngest on the squad. *Not* a mean girl but does enjoy her status, cares a lot about what other people think of her—and by "other people" I mean anyone under the age of consent

JANIS .... age 14, J'NEECE's alter ego. A "good" girl; earnest, sometimes annoyingly so

MOM .... smart, loving, trying to connect with her daughter who has changed since she became a cheerleader

TED .... a scruffy dog who acts like a human, could have been a master thespian if only the gig were open to canines

NOTE: TED can be played by a male or female, but the sense of the character should definitely be male. Utterly un-doglike except when giving a master thespian performance of: A Dog. The lone exception is when he slurps J'NEECE's cheek, sharing with her the genuine affection they used to share before her life became all about cheerleading. J'NEECE and JANIS should be made to look like a mirror image of each other. The actors cast should be approximately the same size so that, appropriately wigged and costumed, they appear to be the same person.

SETTING AND TIME: All action takes place in a 14-year-old girly-girl's bedroom. The set can be as elaborate or as simple as suits the needs of the production. There must be a full-length mirror with no glass. A bed. Chairs or a couch. This can be done simply with draped rehearsal boxes, perhaps a pink beanbag chair.

(LIGHTS up on J'NEECE's bedroom, strewn with signs of popularity and status. Center stage there is a full-length mirror [which actually has no glass, but it should appear to the audience that it does]. J'NEECE stands before the mirror scrutinizing her reflection, turning this way and that. Does her butt look too big? She practices a hair toss, a sexy look...)

MOM *(offstage)*. Janis? Janis!

(J'NEECE is too distracted to reply—she has just noticed what looks like a zit forming on her face. Horrified, she moves up to the mirror, her nose almost touching her reflection, and examines this fresh horror. Her mirrored "reflection" does exactly what J'NEECE does. This is actually JANIS, J'NEECE's alter ego. It should appear to the audience that J'NEECE really is peering at her own reflection.)

MOM *(calls from offstage again, louder, exasperated)*. Janis!! Did you hear me?

J'NEECE *(under her breath, still examining her zit)*. The whole neighborhood heard you. *(Staring at her reflection in the mirror, she swipes on new lipstick—something very loud that clashes with her coloring. During this, she calls to her mom, offstage.)* We have to change it, Mom! I mean, the Trojans? Trojans. Really?

(As J'NEECE works her look in the mirror, pursing her garishly painted lips, her MOM enters, laundry basket in hand. She begins folding J'NEECE's laundry.)

MOM. I wasn't asking about the football team. I was asking if you walked Teddie.

J'NEECE. You think walking the dog is more important than an entire school-wide catastrophe?

MOM. Teddie's used to being walked right after school. But now you don't come home after school—

J'NEECE. Because I had practice. I have to work twice as hard as everyone else—

MOM. Because you're a freshman—you've mentioned it once or twice. *(She hands J'NEECE some clean laundry.)* I'm happy you made the squad—

J'NEECE. No you're not. You think it's stupid.

MOM. But making the squad isn't a good reason to stop walking your dog.

J'NEECE. Could you forget about the dog for one minute? This affects my entire school! We can't be the Trojans!

MOM. Actually, they were amazing, brave soldiers in ancient Greece.

J'NEECE. I don't think so. Trojans are—

MOM *(zeroes in on J'NEECE's lipstick to change the subject)*. What is up with that lipstick?

J'NEECE *(defiant)*. Ashley told me everyone cool is wearing brights this season.

MOM. Since when do you have to do what everyone else does?

J'NEECE. I like it.

MOM *(knows which fights to pick, and when. She shifts)*. You really need to go walk Teddie.

J'NEECE. I'll do it later.

MOM. He's a dog, Janis…

J'NEECE. It's J'NEECE now. I told you.

MOM. But Janis is such a pretty—

J'NEECE. Mom…

MOM. It was your grandmother's—

J'NEECE. No one cool is named Janis. *(A beat.)*

MOM. You were so little when she... Do you remember her?

J'NEECE. She wore this...rose perfume. And she was weird. She used to say words, tell me the part of speech, and then define them for me.

MOM *(a fond memory)*. She did do that.

J'NEECE. Because she thought I was stupid. That's why she did it.

MOM. Oh, sweetie, no—

J'NEECE. And she kept giving me books to read, like that was so much better than gymnastics.

MOM. Did you read any of them?

J'NEECE *(shrugs)*. Face it, I'm nothing like you guys. I just want to be my own person!

MOM *(gently)*. A person who makes her dog wait because all she's thinking about is herself?

J'NEECE *(stung)*. Mean much?

MOM. Teddie can't walk himself.

J'NEECE. What is the biggie about him waiting? That's what dogs do. They wait. Fetch. Roll over...

MOM *(softly chiding)*. Jan— *(remembering)* —J'Neece.

J'NEECE *(getting anxious)*. The first game of the season is tomorrow. I have to practice.

MOM. But—

J'NEECE. They're all waiting for the freshman to mess up, and everyone will laugh at me, Mom! I'll walk Teddie when I'm done. I promise.

MOM. But it isn't fair to—

J'NEECE *(anxiety mounting)*. I'll tell you what isn't fair. Changing the name of our team just because TOM TROJAN'S TERRIFIC TOWING SERVICE paid for our new uniforms and Mr. Tom "Terrific" Trojan himself made us do it! Total abuse of power.

MOM *(dry)*. Well, you wouldn't know anything about that. And a dog.

J'NEECE. Mr. Trojan only did it to try and make his dweeb kid, Arnold, popular. *(She uses thumb and forefinger to make an "L" on her forehead.)* So not happening. But does Arnold's dad get that? Or that every school with a normal team name like the Cougars or the Bears are laughing their butts off at us because we're named after a car-towing service?

MOM. It's really not that bad.

J'NEECE *(her raised eyebrows say: "Wanna bet?" She whirls to the mirror and does a cheer, her "reflection" in perfect synchronicity)*.

> PYTHONS, LIONS, TIGERS AND BEARS!
> TROJANS GOT YOU COVERED
> IN YOUR VERY OWN LAIR!
> G-O-O-O-O
> TROJANS!!!!

(She whirls to her mother, arms folded, as if to say: "See?")

MOM. There are some things you just have to accept, because you don't have the power to change them. Walk Teddie. Not later. Now.

(MOM exits. J'NEECE wavers, a beat of guilt, but anxiety about cheering her first game wins out. She turns to the mirror, practices another cheer, along with her "reflection.")

J'NEECE *(cheering)*.

> READY TROJANS, LET'S GO!
> STRAWBERRY ICE CREAM, BANANA SPLIT!
> TROJANS THINK YOUR TEAM PLAYS LIKE—

(For the first time, her "reflection" doesn't do what J'NEECE does. Instead, she stops, interrupts hastily.)

JANIS. Oh-mi-gosh, you can't say that!

J'NEECE. Spit. I was going to say spit.

JANIS. Liar. Noun. A person who knowingly tells an untruth—

J'NEECE. How would you know? You're a reflection. You can't just…just…freelance!

JANIS *(steps through the mirror, wide-eyed, confidential)*. I went rogue. Don't tell anyone. We have to talk.

J'NEECE. No we don't. You don't exist.

JANIS. First, no cussing in a cheer—very unsportsperson-like. Second, no disrespecting your mom—very undaughterlylike. Third, no making fun of Arnold Trojan—

J'NEECE. Me? I never make fun of anyone!

JANIS. I'm just saying—

J'NEECE. Some guys on the football team are mean to him, maybe, but not me. Like, they'll surround him and fake punch him just to see him flinch. Once, they hung him in a locker…

JANIS. And he fit.

J'NEECE. Wait. You already know all of this. If I saw it, you saw it.

JANIS. It was really mean.

J'NEECE. They were just joking around.

JANIS. At someone else's expense. Someone with less power. And that's?—

J'NEECE *(grudgingly)*. —Mean. I guess. You're right.

JANIS *(exuberant, pulls a large gold sticker star from a pocket and slaps it onto J'NEECE's forehead)*. Gold star! I'm so proud of you!

J'NEECE *(tears it off)*. What is wrong with you?

JANIS. No worries! I've got tons! *(She gleefully pulls fist-fuls of gold star stickers from her pocket, eager to plant another one on J'NEECE.)* Positive feedback is so important—

J'NEECE. Get back in the mirror where you belong, you whack-a-mole!

(During this, TED THE DOG enters on the fly. He walks upright but wears some sort of dog costume. [It should not block his facial expressions or hinder his speech or movement.] A leash trails from his collar. He seems human in every way except...he's a dog. He climbs onto J'NEECE's bed, looming, and manages to overact while panting.)

J'NEECE *(cont'd)*. Down, Teddie! Bad dog!

TED *(thrusts the dangling leash at her.* J'accuse!*)*. Bad human!

JANIS. Sadly, I would have to agree.

J'NEECE. You two are ganging up on me?

TED. Yo, I'm a dog. I've got a pack mentality. Comes with the gig.

JANIS. Anthropologically speaking, that's true. You see—

TED. Save it, savant.

JANIS. Savant. Noun. A person of learning, especially—

TED. Dying to hear the rest. Really. So entertaining. But I'm a caged beast, desperate for a walk. A walk. Get it? It's a euphemism.

J'NEECE. Hey, that was on my vocab quiz!

JANIS *(coaxing)*. And it means...?

TED *(when J'NEECE can't remember...)*. Didn't study? *Quel* shocker.

JANIS. You know what it means. *(Coaxing.)* A mild expression to replace one thought to be offensive...

J'NEECE. If I didn't study, you didn't study!

JANIS. You started to. But then Mack Bart texted you in study hall…

J'NEECE. He is so hot.

JANIS *(even she feels the lure)*. Those dimples when he smiles…

J'NEECE. He's a junior and I'm only a freshman and—

JANIS. Oh-mi-gosh-oh-mi-gosh-oh-mi-gosh! What if he asks you to homecoming?

(The GIRLS share a thrilled gasp at the possibility.)

TED. Female bonding. A beautiful thing. I laughed. I cried. *(Pointedly.)* I wet myself. *(As he lifts a leg—)*

J'NEECE *(grossed out)*. On my bed?

JANIS. He didn't really do it.

TED. Psych! A little *bon mot*.

JANIS. He was joking.

TED. Bilingual canine humor. Picked it up from this smokin' toy poodle.

JANIS. He meets her at the park. After he…you know.

TED. Hey, it's a dirty business but someone's gotta do it. Get it? Dirty "business"? *(He cracks himself up.)*

J'NEECE *(not amused)*. Play dead, Ted!

(TED falls from the bed in a community-theatre-worthy death mime. J'NEECE continues to JANIS, eagerly.)

J'NEECE *(cont'd)*. So we were conversating about Mack…

JANIS. Um, "conversating" isn't a word.

J'NEECE. Yes it is. Ashley says it. And she's head cheerleader!

TED *(rises on an elbow, weighing the difference)*. Head cheerleader, rocket scientist. Head cheerleader, rocket scientist…

J'NEECE. She's nice to everyone and you're supposed to be playing dead!

(TED dramatically "hangs" himself with his leash, tongue hanging out.)

JANIS *(still thinking about what J'NEECE said)*. Not "everyone"…

J'NEECE. Ashley never said one mean thing.

JANIS. But…when her boyfriend was ragging on Arnold, she laughed.

J'NEECE. So? She didn't do anything.

TED. Exactly the point, Your Slowness.

J'NEECE. What was she supposed to do, go: "Oh, making fun of Arnold is so mean!" Publicly humiliate her boy-friend?

TED *(scrambles up and holds out his leash)*. Works for me. Glad we had this little chat.

J'NEECE *(ignores the leash)*. But no girl would do that! It's social suicide.

JANIS *(sits, pats a spot next to her for J'NEECE, who reluctantly joins her)*. J'neece. Sweetie. You're fourteen now. And I think it's time we had "The Talk." See, some things are sins. There are sins of commission and sins of omission…

J'NEECE *(rises hastily)*. I don't believe in doing any of that stuff until I'm married!

TED. Canines don't marry. We mate. Often in the park. With a poodle. On a walk.

J'NEECE. You mean that mangy mutt with the bald spot and the frizz for fur?

TED *(with dignity)*. Well, well. Nice to know you noticed.
Ever since the cheerleading I'm *canina non grata*.

JANIS. He means you don't pay attention—

J'NEECE. I got it.

TED. And my lady-love is not mangy.

J'NEECE. She's also not a poodle.

JANIS. Part poodle. Technically.

J'NEECE. With that funky frizz?

TED. I happen to like the natural look.

J'NEECE *(realizing, horrified)*. It can't be. That mutt be-
longs to—

TED. Arnold Trojan. And he loves her almost as much as I
do. *(Quoting.)* "What is essential is invisible to the eye."

J'NEECE *(a memory comes to her)*. That's from...*The Little
Prince*.

*(JANIS is so excited she pulls out a gold star and moves
to put it on J'NEECE. J'NEECE is not into it.)*

J'NEECE *(cont'd)*. I will seriously hurt you.

JANIS. I'm so proud of you! You—remembered!

J'NEECE. Gramma Janis gave me that book.

JANIS. Because she loved it. And she loved you. Not
because she thought you were—

J'NEECE *(her mind is elsewhere. To TED)*. Wait, you can't
be in love with Arnold's dog. You've been...

*(J'NEECE makes a sipping motion. TED winces, crosses
his paws over his crotch. J'NEECE cracks up.)*

TED. Thank you, O Sensitive One. Why don't I give you a
megaphone, announce it during half-time at the big game
tomorrow. *(He does a cheer, imitating J'NEECE.)*

ONE, TWO, THREE, FOUR
WHO JUST CAN'T SCORE ANYMORE?
P-O-O-O-R TEDDIE!!!!

JANIS *(to J'NEECE)*. You hurt his feelings.

J'NEECE. Oh, come on.

TED. Why not just hang me from a locker? You think making fun of my— *(he makes a snipping motion)* —is so hysterical? Ever consider how I feel? That's rhetorical.

JANIS. Rhetorical. Noun. A question asked when one already knows the—

TED. Excuse me, but I'm on a roll here.

JANIS. Sorry.

TED *(right back into the melodrama)*. You never looked at it from *moi*'s point of view, any more than you looked at it from Arnold's when jocks pretended to hit him just to see him flinch.

J'NEECE *(sincere)*. I did! Look at it from Arnold's point of view, I mean. I wished those guys would stop. But he's a human being. You're just a dog.

JANIS *(to J'NEECE, regretfully speaking the truth)*. And you're just a bully. Sometimes. With Teddie.

TED *(bad televangelist)*. Tell it like it be! Get on the truth train, mah sistuh! Can I get an amen? *(He high-fives JANIS with his paw.)*

J'NEECE *(truly upset)*. But I hate mean people!

JANIS. Not enough to do anything about it. When you have all the power…

J'NEECE. I don't have any power! I'm a freshman!

TED. Ya got power with me, chickadee. Which used to be okay. When I was your pooch, And you were my human.

J'NEECE. I'm still your human!

TED. I could do *Othello* and you wouldn't notice me. I do a killer *Othello*, by the by.

JANIS. Point is, now you only care about power with the cool kids at school.

J'NEECE. I told you. I don't have any—

JANIS. Some of the power, then. But you still stand by and let big guys be deliberately cruel to a little guy.

TED. Like, say, Arnold. Random example.

JANIS. You're a cheerleader!

TED. Emphasis on "leader."

JANIS. Stand up, speak up, do the right thing. If you don't, it's—

J'NEECE. A sin of omission. Not doing something you should have done. Sin of commission is doing something wrong yourself.

JANIS *(realizing)*. You only pretended you didn't know what it meant.

J'NEECE *(proud of herself)*. Psych.

TED. Good one. Almost…Ted-worthy. *(Now they high-five each other.)*

J'NEECE. Bottom line. I'm not calling out the jocks. Even Ashley doesn't have enough power for that. My own mother, a walking case of terminal morality, told me that some things you just have to accept because you don't have enough power to change them.

(J'NEECE's mother enters the other side of the stage. Out of time and space, she can't see or hear the others across the stage. She faces the audience, recalling the conversation with her daughter earlier.)

MOM. Did you read any of them?

(JANIS crosses into MOM's space. MOM is aware of her now, and believes it's J'NEECE. JANIS tries to portray J'NEECE, but her stilted earnestness shines through.)

JANIS. I just want to be my own person.

MOM *(gently)*. A person who makes her dog wait because all she's thinking about is herself? He can't walk himself.

JANIS *(changes J'NEECE's earlier dialogue to what she believes it should have been. To MOM, so earnest)*. You're so right, Mother. I was extremely selfish!

J'NEECE *(objects from across the stage)*. Hey! That is not what I said!

TED. Shhh!

J'NEECE. Please, who writes her lines? I—

TED *(puts a paw over J'NEECE's mouth so she can't speak, enjoying the momentary power over her)*. So satisfying.

(Across the stage, earnest JANIS and MOM continue.)

JANIS. I'll walk Ted right now. The last thing I want to be is a mean person. I'm so sorry, Mother.

(Across the stage, J'NEECE frees her mouth from TED's paw.)

J'NEECE. I'm seriously puking. She makes me sound like a total—

MOM *(to JANIS, across the stage)*. Suck up. The tough lessons, I mean. Learn from them, then do the right thing.

JANIS. I love you, Mother.

MOM *(touched)*. I love you, too.

(MOM exits. JANIS crosses to the others, so proud of herself.)

J'NEECE. You must be kidding.

JANIS. I was just showing you.

J'NEECE. That you're the world's worst actor? *(Looks at TED, at JANIS, at TED again.)* Might be a tie.

TED. Stab me, do I not bleed? *(He mimes stabbing himself in the heart with a dagger.)*

JANIS. That you had the power to do it differently. You still do.

TED *(grandly)*. "To educate a man in the mind but not in morals is to educate a menace to society."

J'NEECE. You did not just make that up.

TED. From now on, do not call me Teddie. Or Ted. Call me…Theodore.

J'NEECE. Alvin's brother? You want to be a chipmunk?

TED. Theodore as in "Roosevelt." One of the greatest presidents of these United States.

J'NEECE & JANIS. The twenty-sixth. *(They share a beat of mutual regard.)*

TED *(to J'NEECE)*. Nothin' for nothin,' but truth is…I kinda miss my human. It makes me a tad cranky.

JANIS. People—and pets—who feel powerless get so angry, and they either take it out on themselves, or find a way to fight back, or—

J'NEECE. Do you know how annoying it is? That you think you know everything? You sound just like my grandmother.

JANIS. That's who I got it from.

J'NEECE. Well bully for you. It's still irritating.

JANIS. Do you remember what she used to say to you? "I will teach you how to be excellent, my Jan-ell-ah…

J'NEECE & JANIS. …Because you are capable of excellence." *(A beat, the GIRLS regard each other, two sides of the same person.)*

J'NEECE *(realizing, some awe)*. I do remember.

TED. Well, "Bully-bully!" You know who said that?

J'NEECE. Me. Like two seconds ago.

TED. You said "bully." Theodore Roosevelt said "bully-bully."

JANIS. Bully. Noun. One who is habitually cruel to those who are weaker.

J'NEECE. Or "Bully." Adjective. Meaning…excellent. How weird is that?

TED. The question is: Which kind of "bully" do you want to be?

JANIS. Gramma Janis just wanted you to be the best you—we—could be.

J'NEECE. You think?

JANIS. I went rogue for you, didn't I? I know.

J'NEECE *(a beat, as she decides)*. I'll try.

JANIS *(glee)*. That is so—

J'NEECE. But I'm not giving up cheerleading. And no way I'm changing my name back to Janis.

TED *(quoting Shakespeare)*. "What's in a name?" *(Both GIRLS stare at him blankly.)* Never mind. You're young. You've got time to learn. I'm ten. In human years, I'm Grandma Moses.

J'NEECE *(a beat, as she recalls her very real love for her dog. Then, from the heart)*. I couldn't stand it if anything happened to you.

TED *(ditto)*. Back atcha. *(He produces a rose from somewhere and hands it to J'NEECE. Then he slurps her cheek in a wet doggy kiss. And she lets him.)* I'm long in the tooth, and short on time. Also, my bladder isn't what it used to be. We're walking?

J'NEECE. Right this minute.

TED. Excellent. Because after I…"take care of business," I have a date with a semi-bald, frizzy-furred, four-legged angel. If you laugh—

JANIS. We won't.

J'NEECE. Promise. I remember. The smell of roses. *(She inhales the flower's scent again.)* "What is essential is invisible to the eye." We won't let anyone else laugh, either.

TED. Really? You'd do that for me?

J'NEECE. Really.

JANIS. I love happy endings!

(J'NEECE and JANIS hug. They are one, integrated girl.)

TED. Cut, cut, cut. Way too sweet. Diabetic coma territory. And the performances—

JANIS *(interrupting)*. Theodore?

TED. I'll be giving copious notes.

J'NEECE. Really. Well—

JANIS & J'NEECE. Bully-Bully!

(They link arms and paws, with much leash-lasso spinning and funky moves from TED, they sing and dance their way offstage to the rock classic, "Wooly-Bully," changed here to "Bully-Bully."

NOTE: Because this makes it a parody, it is considered fair and legal usage.)

END OF PLAY

The Bully Pulpit

By Dwayne Hartford

CHARACTERS

BARBARA.................a very determined high-school senior
KATIE..Barbara's best friend
BRIAN...Katie's boyfriend
LEE.................a member of Barbara's campaign committee
JENNY ....a shy teenager (from her appearance, one
            assumes that she is a social outcast in high school)

SETTING AND TIME: The play takes place today. There are two locations: the stage of a high-school auditorium and the family room at Katie's house.

WORDS TO PONDER: *"I suppose my critics will call that preaching, but I have got such a bully pulpit!"*

– Theodore Roosevelt

Scene 1: The Stage

(BARBARA is standing at a podium.)

BARBARA. ...so if you are looking for someone to just organize bake sales and plan school dances, don't vote for me. But, if you want somebody who will make a difference, then I am the one. I want to make Theodore Roosevelt High School a safe environment where everybody is free to learn and to be themselves. If you agree, vote for me, Barbara Kennedy, for senior class president. Thank you.

Scene 2: Katie's Family Room

(A sofa, a TV, a table with chairs. LEE sits at the table working on a laptop, KATIE sits on the sofa texting, BRIAN is operating a PlayStation controller.)

BRIAN. Yes! Did you see that?

KATIE. What?

BRIAN. I just won again.

KATIE. Good. Now can we talk about the campaign?

BRIAN. Who are you texting?

KATIE. I was tweeting about the rally tomorrow morning. We've got to build interest.

BRIAN. I'm hungry. Does your mom have any more of those cookies?

KATIE. You ate them all yesterday. Now, Barbara will be here in a minute, and she wanted us to start before she got here.

BRIAN. Doesn't make a lot of sense starting the campaign meeting without the candidate. What's Barb doing, anyway? School let out almost an hour ago.

KATIE. I don't know. She said she had something to do. I think she's nervous about tomorrow's rally.

BRIAN. I didn't think she ever got nervous. Barb is like a machine.

KATIE. She isn't a machine. And don't call her Barb. You know she hates that.

LEE. OK, I've done a new poster. What do you think? *(He shows the other two the laptop.)*

KATIE. "Koo-Koo for Kennedy." Cute.

LEE. You don't like it?

KATIE. I don't think it's what Barbara wants.

LEE. Oh.

KATIE. It's not very dignified.

LEE. I thought the campaign could use a little, I don't know, something…

KATIE. Something what?

LEE. Fun. I mean, don't get me wrong, I think the whole anti-bullying thing is great, but—don't you think we're being a little too serious all the time?

KATIE. But that's what Barbara is trying to say—that being class president is more than just about having fun. She wants to change things.

BRIAN. That's great, Katie, but Lee is right. Barb-ar-a needs to lighten up a little.

KATIE. You guys just don't get it. She's been my best friend since…

BRIAN. …since kindergarten. I know.

KATIE. This is really important to her.

BRIAN. I know. We all know how badly she wants to be class president.

KATIE. It's because of what she wants to accomplish.

BRIAN. Sure it is.

KATIE. What's that supposed to mean?

BRIAN. Nothing. Nothing.

KATIE. You promised you wouldn't say anything to upset her.

BRIAN. She's not here.

KATIE. Brian!

BRIAN. I won't.

KATIE. I know she can be intense, but it's only because she cares.

BRIAN. I know.

KATIE. She has really, really been there for me.

BRIAN. I think you are more than even on that score.

KATIE. Brian…

BRIAN. OK. Truce. I promise to be on good behavior.

KATIE. She'll make a great class president.

BRIAN. I agree. If anyone can get things done, it's Barbara. OK? *(He hugs KATIE and kisses her.)*

LEE. Hello? The third wheel is right over here.

KATIE. Sorry, Lee.

LEE. Geez. Get a room, why don't you?

BRIAN. Yeah. Yeah.

LEE. I'm just jealous. It's only me and my laptop.

BRIAN. Maybe our future class president can find you someone. Maybe that could be part of her agenda.

LEE. What a great idea! All she has to do is tell someone to go out with me, and they'll have to do it. After all, nobody says no to Barbara.

BRIAN. That's right. Nobody says no to Barbara.

LEE. Look at me. I'm spending how many afternoons making posters and flyers. Yes, Barbara. Yes.

KATIE. It's not true. People can… I say no to her.

(LEE and BRIAN look at each other.)

KATIE *(cont'd).* I do! What?

LEE. Uh-huh.

KATIE. What do you mean, uh-huh?

BRIAN. Katie. I'm crazy about you, but you cannot say no to Barbara.

KATIE. I can too.

BRIAN. If only that were true. Just once I'd like to hear you say no to her. Just once.

KATIE. I can! I have!

(BARBARA and JENNY enter. JENNY stays back from the group.)

BARBARA. You can and have what?

KATIE. Nothing.

BRIAN. We were just—uh—thinking about ways to—uh—give the campaign some…

LEE. Some pizzazz.

BARBARA. Pizzazz?

KATIE. They were just goofing around. Who's this?

BARBARA. This is the newest member of the campaign committee, Jenny Brown.

BRIAN. Hey, Jenny. You're in band, right?

JENNY. Yes.

BARBARA. Jenny plays flute.

JENNY. Oboe.

BARBARA. Oboe. Right. She's going to get us the music vote.

KATIE. Great. That's great.

BARBARA. So, team, let's hear your big plan for the campaign.

BRIAN. Our big plan?

BARBARA. Pizzazz?

LEE. Well… *(He holds up the laptop.)*

BARBARA. "Koo-Koo for Kennedy." Cute.

KATIE. I told you she wouldn't like it.

BARBARA. No. I think it's great. I think it's really great to treat mental illness like a joke.

LEE. What?

BRIAN. It's just a campaign slogan.

KATIE. He didn't mean it that way.

BARBARA. Words matter. That's what I'm trying to get people to understand. No one has the right to make another person feel bad about themselves. That's what this is all about.

BRIAN. OK. OK. We get it.

LEE. I suppose "Wacko" is out of the question.

BARBARA. What?

LEE. Kidding. How's this? "Wild for Kennedy." That's not making fun of anyone, is it?

KATIE. That's better.

BRIAN. So, Jenny, how do you and Barbara know each other?

BARBARA. Oh, Jenny and I were in Spanish class together freshman year. Right, Jenny?

JENNY. Yeah.

BARBARA. We ran into each other today and she wanted to help with the campaign. Right?

JENNY. Ah. Yeah.

BARBARA. And she knows something about bullying. Don't you, Jenny?

JENNY. What?

BARBARA. She's had to put up with a lot, just because of…who she is. Haven't you?

KATIE. Barbara…

BARBARA. What? You feel uncomfortable, Katie? Well, good. You should. You all should. This campaign is about Jenny. Jenny and everyone like her.

BRIAN. OK, but maybe she doesn't want to talk about it.

BARBARA. Maybe you don't want to talk about it, Brian. But Jenny is here because she's sick of it, aren't you, Jenny?

JENNY. I thought you needed help with…I don't think I…

BARBARA. Don't! Don't let these guys intimidate you.

BRIAN. Who's intimidating?

BARBARA *(goes to JENNY and puts her arm around her)*. Jenny is the bravest person I know. And you know why?

Because she is ready to stand up proud in front of people and say, "Stop!"

KATIE. What?

BARBARA. That's right, isn't it, Jenny? That's why you're here, isn't it?

JENNY. I've...I've got to go.

BARBARA. Don't go. We've got to talk. I just had a great idea.

BRIAN. Ah. And here it is.

KATIE. What's your idea?

BARBARA. I'm thinking that at tomorrow morning's campaign rally, Jenny should stand next to me, and together we'll call out the people who've been bullying her. Daring them to acknowledge what they've done. Challenging them to step forward and, in view of the whole school, to apologize.

BRIAN. Apologize? You've got to be kidding.

BARBARA. Why not? We'll shame them into treating Jenny and everyone like her with the respect that they deserve.

KATIE. Do you really think it would work?

BARBARA. I think it'll put them on notice.

LEE *(to JENNY)*. You'd do this?

JENNY. I...you didn't tell me...

BARBARA. I didn't tell you, because I just thought of it.

BRIAN. Yeah, right.

KATIE. Brian.

BARBARA. And what is your problem?

BRIAN. My problem? Well, one—it won't work, and two— it'll humiliate her.

BARBARA. It won't humiliate her. It'll give her a feeling of self-worth that she hasn't felt in a long time.

BRIAN. Nice.

BARBARA. What?

BRIAN. You're going to use her to get votes.

BARBARA. I'm not using her! I'm helping her.

BRIAN. By standing her in front of the whole school and having her beg people to be nice to her?

BARBARA. She won't be begging. She'll be demanding. And I'll be standing right there beside her. Maybe you don't believe it, but I am really, really there for her.

BRIAN. This is a bad idea. Katie, Lee, back me up on this.

JENNY. I've got to go.

BRIAN. Good. Run as fast as you can.

BARBARA. No! You're not the one who's leaving, Jenny! He is!

KATIE. Barbara…

BRIAN. Are you kicking me out of my own girlfriend's house?

KATIE. You guys…

BRIAN. Katie, tell me you think that this rally thing is a bad idea! You do, don't you?

KATIE. Well…

BARBARA. Don't let him put words in your mouth, Katie.

BRIAN. What? Look who's talking!

BARBARA. I'm standing up for my friends, thank you very much.

BRIAN. No you're not. Katie, you see what's happening here?

BARBARA. There he goes, Katie. I knew he'd eventually try to force you to choose between us. He's been jealous of our friendship forever.

BRIAN. What?

BARBARA. Admit it, Brian. You can't stand that Katie has a best friend other than you.

BRIAN. Barbara, I've put up with you because of Katie, but you really… *(Pointing to the laptop.)* Lee, you have the right idea, just cut out the word "for." Koo-Koo Kennedy.

BARBARA. Name calling. How very mature of you. You can leave now.

BRIAN. Katie, do you want me to go?

KATIE. Brian…

BRIAN. I know. She's been your best friend since kindergarten. News flash, Katie. She's not your best friend. She's not even a friend. You are her best friend. And that's it.

KATIE. That's not…

BARBARA. How dare you?

BRIAN. Butt out, Barb! Katie, say no to her. Just say no. For once. For me.

(Silence.)

KATIE. Brian. Maybe you should go.

LEE. But…he's on the committee.

BRIAN. Not anymore. I'm out of here. *(He leaves.)*

BARBARA. Good.

JENNY. I'm going, too.

BARBARA. But…you'll do the rally tomorrow, right?

JENNY. I can't.

BARBARA. Of course you can.

JENNY. No. I can't! I won't! Look. I don't really know you, and I definitely don't know what's going on here, so I'm just going to choose to believe that you want to do this for all the right reasons. I'm going to choose to believe that you really think I need your help, and that you can—in your own twisted way—make my life better. Yeah. I'm going to believe that. And I'm going to leave now, before you say something that proves me wrong.

BARBARA. Well…

JENNY. No!

(This silences BARBARA. JENNY leaves.)

LEE. Wow.

KATIE. What?

LEE. She said no. *(BARBARA glares at him.)* I've got to go, too. I'll finish the poster at home and email you. *(He takes the laptop and leaves.)*

BARBARA. Well, your boyfriend has really sabotaged my campaign, hasn't he?

KATIE. He didn't…

BARBARA. Didn't what? He's always hated me. He hates strong women.

KATIE. What?

BARBARA. That's why he likes you. I can't believe how much control he has over you.

KATIE. Control?

BARBARA. Everybody sees it, Katie. You know what he is, don't you?

KATIE. What?

BARBARA. A bully.

KATIE. Brian?

BARBARA. It's true! You know what? To heck with Jenny. She thinks I'm twisted? Well, she can go without my help. But you. You'll stand next to me at that rally. You'll stand there, and we'll dare Brian to admit to the way he treats you.

KATIE. I can't do that.

BARBARA. Yes, you can! I want to do this for you. Katie, I am really, really there for you.

KATIE. I know, but…

BARBARA. It's a great idea. It'll be good for you. And it'll be good for…the school!

KATIE. He doesn't…bully…

BARBARA. You just can't see it, because you're blind to his faults.

KATIE. I'm not...

BARBARA. It's a problem you have.

KATIE. I don't think...

BARBARA. I'm sorry if it hurts, but I'm your best friend. I know you better than anyone. People take advantage of you and you let them.

KATIE. That's...that's not true.

BARBARA. Yes, it is! But it's going to stop. I'm going to help you.

KATIE. You think people take advantage of me?

BARBARA. I've told you that a million times. You don't stick up for yourself, that's all. But it's OK. That's why you have me.

KATIE. But, Brian...

BARBARA. Katie! Who has been there for you since kindergarten?

KATIE. You have.

BARBARA. And I'll be there for you tomorrow morning at the rally.

KATIE. It doesn't feel right.

BARBARA. Well it is! Don't be such a wimp for once in your life! Grow a backbone, would you?

KATIE. Grow a backbone...

BARBARA. Exactly! Tomorrow morning you are finally going to stand up to the bully. End of discussion!

(BARBARA and KATIE look at each other. KATIE doesn't speak.)

Scene 3: The Podium in the School Auditorium

(BARBARA stands at a podium. KATIE stands at her side.)

BARBARA. This campaign has really opened my eyes to the fact that bullying is happening all over this campus. Bullies take many forms. They can be strangers, or they can be friends—even boyfriends. This here is Katie. Today she and I are going to call out her bully. Aren't we, Katie? *(Pause.)* Speak up, Katie.

KATIE. No.

BARBARA. No? that's right, Katie. Say no to bullying!

KATIE. No, Barbara.

BARBARA. Katie?

KATIE. I'm standing up. No, Barbara. No!

END OF PLAY

A Bully There Be

By Lisa Dillman

CHARACTERS

SERVING WENCH
JESTER
PRINCE

SETTING: A royal palace in a land very far away.

TIME: Once upon a…

(Enter SERVING WENCH. She carries a large hunk of raw meat.)

WENCH *(confidentially to the audience)*.
> There be a bully in this palace.
> A bully, full of stink and malice.
> Big he's not, nor strong at all,
> But he's a bully still, withal.

(Enter JESTER on the run. He wears a cap and bells, a suit of motley, the works. He has a black eye. He skids to a stop as SERVING WENCH steps into his path and holds out the raw meat.)

WENCH.
> Here, fool, do take this cut of beef
> And to thine eye bring sweet relief.

JESTER.
> Good serving wench, how kind thou art.
> *(Aside.)* As well as lovely, sweet and smart…

(JESTER moons at her, one hand over his heart, the other pressing the steak to his eye. SERVING WENCH blushes prettily, sweetly, smartly.)

WENCH.
> How came thee by this massive shiner?

JESTER *(whiney)*.
> I'd tell thee, but I'm not a whiner.

WENCH.
> No need to tell for yea in truth
> I know it was the prince, forsooth.

JESTER *(ashamed)*.
> Aye. 'Twas he.
> He did but catch me unawares
> Else I'd've kicked him down the stairs.

(SERVING WENCH nods sympathetically, doubtfully, and adjusts the steak on JESTER's eye.)

JESTER.
> A blinding blow he dealt mine face
> Else I'd've clocked him with mine mace.

WENCH.
> Of course thou wouldst've!
> *(SOUND of drums.)*
> But hark, I hear the drums!

JESTER.

> And something wicked this way comes.

PRINCE *(roaring from offstage)*. Where is my *FOOL*!

WENCH.

> 'Tis not just that he's mean and violent
> He also screams; he's *never* silent …
Let us away! Hurry!

> *(SERVING WENCH pulls JESTER around a corner where they crouch.)*

JESTER. I can take this no more. He steals from me my very wit.

WENCH.

> Nay! Thou art the king's beloved jester.
> Thou mustn't let thy talents fester.
> As stand-ups go, there be none better.
> Thy shtick quite sets the court a-titter.

JESTER.

Alas. No longer.

> Where once I earned a thousand chuckles,
> This prince arrives and my wit buckles.
> He's slaughtered my timing—
> Laid waste to my rhymes…
> And he ne'er…umm…he ne'er…?

WENCH.

> …allows thee sweet good times?

JESTER. Nay, nay… He slaughtered my timing, laid waste to my rhymes…and he never…uhhhhh?

WENCH.
　　…suffers one little bit for his crimes?

JESTER.
　　See thee now how he hath unmirthed me?
　　Stripped me of my sense of fun.
　　And left me neither joke nor pun.

WENCH. Oh dear! 'Tis worse than ever I thought!

JESTER *(holding out a shaking hand)*.
　　My hands shake.
　　My very tongue goes dry.
　　If my jesting pleaseth not the king,
　　Then I must give up everything.

WENCH. The King doth *love* thee. 'Tis but this heinous prince who…

JESTER. Gone my suit of motley…gone my cap and bells—

PRINCE *(offstage)*. Heeere, Jester, Jester, Jester! Here, boy! C'mon boy!

JESTER.
　　Anon he comes and so I fly
　　Lest he do black mine other eye.
　　(Handing the meat back to SERVING WENCH.)
　　Good wench, I thank thee for this steak.

WENCH.
　　Nay, keep it, lest thy nose he break.

JESTER
    'Tis goodly counsel, no mistake.
    (He pockets the meat.)

WENCH. Get thee gone! I shall distract His Highness Junior.

JESTER *(to the audience confidentially).*
    Stay where ye are; don't move an inch.
    For yonder comes the heinous prince!

WENCH *(to JESTER).* Art thou still *here*?

(She shoves him offstage. PRINCE enters, yelling after the JESTER.)

PRINCE. So? Make me laugh, funny man! Aye, thou had *better* run! For verily thy punch lines do sucketh most painfully!

(Someone HISSES from the audience. The PRINCE turns very slowly and appraises the audience à la Taxi Driver.*)*

PRINCE *(cont'd).*
    What art thou lookin' at…?
    Art thou talkin' to me?
    Art *thou*…talkin' to *me*?
    For verily, I be the only one here.

(SERVING WENCH meanwhile attempts to tiptoe offstage. PRINCE suddenly turns and grabs her, begins hitting her in the head with her own arm.)

PRINCE *(cont'd)*. How now? Uh-oh! Wench, stop hitting thyself! Stop hitting thyself, Wench!

WENCH.
>   Good prince, I beg thee, drop my arm.
>   I've never done thee any harm.
>   I'm but a simple serving wench—
>   There be no need my arm to clench.

PRINCE.
>   I care not what thou doest or sayest
>   'Tis only thou art in my way…est.

(BOTH note the forced rhyme. He gives her a little shove.)

WENCH. I go, I go. But first… Beggin' thy pardon, Prince Cloddendork.

PRINCE *(grabbing her ear)*. *What didst thou call me?*

WENCH. I…! I…?

PRINCE. Spew it forth, stout wench!

WENCH. Stout?! I'll have thee know, I weigh but five stone soaking wet!—

PRINCE. 'Tis only an *expression*. Now. Speak. How came thee to call me by that wretched name?

WENCH. I called thee by the name thy father gave thee.

PRINCE *(low, dangerous)*. And what name was that again?

WENCH. "Cloddendork," Highness?

PRINCE. Nay! I am "Junior," First son of Engeldorf the Taciturn.

WENCH.
>   That is thy *nickname*, thou speakest true.
>   But there is a more *official* you.

For at thy birth when fled the stork
Thy parents dubbed thee Cloddendork.

PRINCE. Impudent scullery baggage, how didst thou come
to know of this?

WENCH.
    Thy *name*, good sir?
    Why, 'tis as legend in this palace.
    Just as thy sister's name is Alice.
    Blame me not for thine own name!
    (Methinks it suits thee just the same.)

PRINCE. Why thou I oughta—! Thou thinkest me a clod?
WENCH. Nay sir.
PRINCE. A dork then?

(He gives her a noogie. She squeals.)

WENCH. Nay, not at all.
PRINCE. Why oh why doth everyone hate me so? Am I not
handsome?
WENCH. Ehh. Thou art not bad. Thy looks thwart thee not.
PRINCE. And am I not brilliant and well read?
WENCH. I know not.
PRINCE. Well, I am! And am I not charming?
WENCH. I would not call thee charming.
PRINCE. But I am witty. Thou canst deny it.
WENCH. Else thou shall behead me?
PRINCE. I might.
WENCH. I imagine many of thy father's subjects have
proclaimed thy wit when it was put to them thus.
PRINCE. Most are pleased to tell me that I put forth some
awfully good wisecracks. And if nothing else, I'm funnier

than that lame jester… Thou may now feel free to agree with me.

WENCH. Ahh. Now I see. Thou dost not want the truth after all.

PRINCE. Aye, the truth! Forsooth!

WENCH. Thou wilt not clout me if I tell thee true?

PRINCE. Nay. Scout's honor.

WENCH. Thy fingers are crossed. *(PRINCE uncrosses his fingers.)* Keep thy hands where I can see them. All right. Here 'tis. Thou art sour, ill tempered, spiteful, mean, and petty. Thou kickest thine own mongrel and starvest thy pet hamster nigh unto death. Thou art rude and selfish. Thou chewest with thy mouth open and fail to excuse thyself even when thou belchest most profoundly—

PRINCE. But—?

WENCH. I've not finished. Thou art a litterbug and a pottymouth. Thy hygiene is appalling—

PRINCE. But—?

WENCH. Thou takest pleasure in terrorizing those charged with waiting upon thee; thou seekest out opportunities to assault thy most loyal subjects—

PRINCE. But?—

WENCH. But *what*?

PRINCE. Do thou not…?

WENCH. Do I not what?

PRINCE. Do thou not know I am so very different on the inside? *(Beat.)*

WENCH. The inside. Where would that be? Show it me.

PRINCE. I cannot. 'Tis…well. 'Tis on the…*inside*, naturally.

WENCH. Thou keepest it very safe from others. That is thy trouble. Thou art too mistrustful. Thy fear undoes thee.

PRINCE. Ha! I fear no one. I am the most feared personage in this palace.

WENCH. The fact that others fear thee doth not mean thou art not thyself fearful.

PRINCE. Oh?

WENCH. Yea. Verily.

PRINCE. Thou art deluded.

WENCH. Then tell me how thou art feeling at this very moment.

PRINCE. Annoyed.

WENCH. Nay. Thou art afraid. And now?

PRINCE. Actually getting a bit angry now...

WENCH. Thou art terrified.

PRINCE. I must warn thee. I'm now inching toward wrathful.

WENCH. Thou art *petrified,* Prince Cloddendork. Petrified of thy parents, thy subjects, thy servants, yes, even I...me...I. Thou fearest thou art ridiculous which, sadly, makes thee behave in a most ridiculous fashion. And oh dear, what if I should *ever* laugh at thee? *(She titters annoyingly.)* How dost thou like that?

PRINCE. I like it not. Cease and desist or heads will roll. Literally.

WENCH. Sadly, that is thy answer for everything. *Adieu,* my liege, for now I have a most pressing engagement with my scullery brush, which is, sad to say, much better company than thee. Thou. Thee.

PRINCE. All right. But thou wilt walk round the garden with me later in the evening air.

WENCH. Nay, I will not.

PRINCE. I command it.

WENCH. Even so, my answer is nay.

PRINCE. Say yea.

WENCH. Nay.

PRINCE. *Yea.*

WENCH. For the last time: *NAY.*

PRINCE. Then I shall behead thee.

WENCH. Very well, do. *(Bending her head in his direction.)* Behead me already! What art thou waiting for?

PRINCE. I *love* thee! *(Stunned, he claps both hands over his mouth.)*

WENCH. *What?*

PRINCE. I…love thee?

WENCH. If that be true…

PRINCE. 'Tis. I assure thee. Thy lips, thy hair, thy sweet be-dimpled chin, I love thee with all my heart.

WENCH. Prove it.

PRINCE. Fine. I shall kiss thee. Come hither.

WENCH. Nay, for that would give thee *pleasure*. Thou wilt have to do something far more difficult to prove thy *love*.

PRINCE. Command me, O goddess of the scullery.

WENCH. Thou must summon the jester and solemnly promise never to slap, punch, kick, poke, pinch, prod, thump, strike, beat, trip, or otherwise harm him in any way in the future. And then tell him thou art sorry for the many times thou hast harmed him in the past. If thou doest this small thing, I *might* be persuaded to promenade with thee in the garden, as you suggested, at dusk when the sun is sliding down the sky… Thou hesitatest? Thou lovest me not!

PRINCE. Nay, verily I do and have for years. I am fair sick with it.

WENCH *(softening a bit)*. Shall I call the jester hither then?

(PRINCE undergoes a quiet, rather painful transition that contorts his whole body. His eyes cross and his face turns crimson. Finally…)

PRINCE. All right, all right.

(SERVING WENCH whistles sharply between her teeth. Immediately the JESTER runs on. When he sees PRINCE, he skids to a halt and begins to quake.)

WENCH. Jester, the prince has something to say to thee. *(JESTER cringes in anticipation.)* Say on, Prince.

(PRINCE and SERVING WENCH have a brief, intense stare fight, which she finally wins.)

PRINCE. Fool, I promise... I promise I will never slap, punch, kick, poke, pinch, prod, thump, strike, beat, trip, or otherwise harm thee in future.

WENCH. And?

PRINCE. And I am heartily sorry if I have caused thee any pain in the past. Wilt thou accept my apology and forgive me?

(Stunned, JESTER stares for a few beats until SERVING WENCH nudges him sharply.)

JESTER. Forgive thee? Of course! Why, 'tisn't even a question. Thy apology is most humbly accepted a thousandfold. Thou art forgiven. I forgive thee. Oh, what a day! Yes! I accept with great pleasure, Highness. After all, what is the world without forgiveness and—

PRINCE. Right. And now I'm certain thou must be off to somewhere.

JESTER. Not really.

PRINCE. Surely thou hast some pressing foolery and jesting to attend to.

JESTER. Nah, I'm pretty open.

WENCH *(taking the PRINCE's hand)*. Off you go, Jesty. The prince and I have some promenading to do. 'Tis nearly dusk and the sun doth slide low.

(They moon at each other. Then, hand in hand, they exit.)

JESTER *(looking after them)*. Why, thou little gold digger. *(He takes the beefsteak out his pocket and presses it to his eye. Turns to the audience.)*

> A bully there was within this palace
> A bully full and spite and malice.
> But life is good and love is strange
> And even bullies sometimes change.
> Time will tell, and who can say?
> Perhaps some good was done this day.
> *(He shrugs.)*

Ehh. Perhaps.

(He sighs. Does a little jesterly dance step. Sighs again.)

BLACKOUT

END OF PLAY

A Bunch of Clowns

By Sandra Fenichel Asher

CHARACTERS (m or w)

RINGMASTER
CLOWNS .... (at least 3, 6 would be better,
and a bunch more is better still)
NEW KID

SETTING AND TIME: A school…a circus…no, a school…
no, a circus. Take your pick. Any time.

WORDS TO PONDER: *There is a foggy borderland
between clowning around and cruelty, good-natured teasing
and bullying. The action of this play begins on the benign
side of that borderland, enters it, and ventures across to the
other side. Director and actors are encouraged to explore
the subtle differences of intent and action and how best to
dramatize them.*

*(Circus MUSIC. RINGMASTER enters, strutting pom-
pously in full clown costume with fright wig and red
nose, but differentiated from the others by a top hat, whip
and domineering personality. RINGMASTER is followed
on by a bunch of CLOWNS who shuffle along in an
awkward huddle, grinning foolishly. Some carry clown
assault paraphernalia: slapsticks, foam bats or sawed-off
Pool Noodles, seltzer bottles or other spritzers. ALL
circle the stage, RINGMASTER in the lead. With each*

*crack of RINGMASTER's whip, CLOWNS interrupt their
shuffle to execute a small, hiccup-like jump of surprise,
after which they immediately resume their huddle and
grinning. As RINGMASTER and CLOWNS approach UC
an unremarkable NEW KID enters downstage, in street
clothes, with backpack. NEW KID crosses stage, looking
first-day disoriented. Upon seeing NEW KID,
RINGMASTER brings CLOWN huddle to an abrupt stop.)*

RINGMASTER *(cracking whip)*. HALT!

*(MUSIC, CLOWNS and NEW KID stop short. ALL except
RINGMASTER react to whip with a small jump of
surprise. Then—)*

RINGMASTER *(cont'd)*. Hey! New Kid!
NEW KID. Who, me?
RINGMASTER. You're new, aren't you?
NEW KID. Yes.
RINGMASTER. Right! You're a kid, aren't you?
NEW KID. Yes.
RINGMASTER. Right! So that's why I'm calling you New
     Kid.
NEW KID. Oh. But—
RINGMASTER. You've run away to join the circus,
     haven't you?
NEW KID. No, I'm here for the first day of school—
RINGMASTER. School. Circus. Circus. School. Take your
     pick. What's in a name?
NEW KID. Well, actually—
RINGMASTER. Nothing! So step right up! Let's have a
     look at you, New Kid. We've got to figure out where you
     fit into the act.
NEW KID. Oh...okay...I guess.

(NEW KID hesitantly moves a bit closer to RING-MASTER and grinning, huddled CLOWNS.)

RINGMASTER. Here's how it goes, New Kid. You want to be in the act, you have three choices. Allow us to demonstrate.

(RINGMASTER cracks whip. OTHERS jump as before, then three CLOWNS quickly line up to demonstrate.)

RINGMASTER *(cont'd)*. You can play the Bully...

(RINGMASTER cracks whip. ALL jump. CLOWN #1 strikes a tough pose.)

RINGMASTER *(cont'd)*. You can play the Bullied...

(Same business. CLOWN #2 strikes an intimidated pose.)

RINGMASTER *(cont'd)*. Or you can play the Bystander...

(Same business. CLOWN #3 strikes a nonchalant pose.)

RINGMASTER *(cont'd)*. Do it!

(RINGMASTER cracks whip. OTHERS jump. Then CLOWN #1 whacks CLOWN #2 on the back and strikes a gloating pose. CLOWN #2 falls flat on the floor and stays there, cowered and whimpering. CLOWN #3 turns away and assumes a nonchalant pose.)

CLOWN #3. I din't see nothin'.

(CLOWNS #1, #2 and #3 freeze.)

NEW KID. That's it?

RINGMASTER. A brief sample, New Kid. Three choices. So listen up. *(Steps beside CLOWN #3.)* Choice Number Three is essentially boring. You don't get to do anything new, ever. You're a Bystander. What kind of a life is that?

NEW KID. You're always standing by.

RINGMASTER. Right!

(RINGMASTER nudges CLOWN #2 with a toe. CLOWN #2 whimpers, then freezes.)

RINGMASTER *(cont'd).* Now, some might disagree, but I think Choice Number Two is a lot more interesting. *(Another nudge, another whimper.)* You never know what's going to happen next. *(Another nudge, another whimper.)* Your days are full.

NEW KID. But they all suck.

RINGMASTER. Right! *(Steps beside gloating BULLY.)* Choice Number One, though, now that's creative. You get to think up new stuff all the time. The sky's the limit!

(RINGMASTER cracks whip. OTHERS jump. ALL but NEW KID scramble back into huddle.)

RINGMASTER *(cont'd).* Do it!

(Another CRACK of the whip. OTHERS jump. Then CLOWNS take turns offering bullying suggestions and forming a series of tableaux to illustrate each of them with a BULLY, BULLIED and BYSTANDER. Lines and actions may be divided among additional CLOWNS as needed. Though the intensity increases, at this point the tactics are still presented as humorous clown antics.)

CLOWN #1. The spritz…
CLOWN #2. The pinch…
CLOWN #3. The poke…
CLOWN #1. The shove…
CLOWN #2. The clobber…
CLOWN #3. The name call…
CLOWN #1. The phone call…
CLOWN #2. The elbow…
CLOWN #3. The knee…
CLOWN #1. The slur…
CLOWN #2. The slam…
CLOWN #3. The trip-up…
CLOWN #1. The shun…
CLOWN #2. The meet-me-at-the-movies-and-I-never-show-up…
CLOWN #3. The come-to-the-party-in-an-empty-lot…
CLOWN #1. The tell-me-your-secret-and-I'll-share-it-with-the-world—
RINGMASTER *(cracks whip. ALL jump)*. Halt!

(CLOWNS scurry back into grinning huddle.)

RINGMASTER *(cont'd, to NEW KID)*. Get the picture?
NEW KID. I do! Greatest show on earth!
RINGMASTER. Right! So what'll it be, New Kid?

(RINGMASTER cracks whip. OTHERS jump. Then CLOWNS #1, #2, and #3 assume the BULLY, BULLIED, and BYSTANDER poses as before.)

RINGMASTER *(cont'd)*. Choice Number Three? Choice Number Two? Or Choice Number One?
NEW KID. Choice Number One, of course!
RINGMASTER. Right!

(RINGMASTER cracks whip; ALL jump; CIRCUS MUSIC plays. CLOWNS set aside NEW KID's backpack and help NEW KID don a clown suit, red nose and fright wig. NEW KID reports to RINGMASTER for duty. RING-MASTER cracks whip; OTHERS jump; MUSIC stops short.)

RINGMASTER *(cont'd)*. Do it!

(RINGMASTER cracks whip again; OTHERS jump, and following montage ensues: CLOWNS line up in pairs of BULLIEDS and BYSTANDERS. NEW KID pulls a bullying maneuver on FIRST BULLIED, who freezes in cowered position.)

CLOWN AS FIRST BYSTANDER *(strikes a nonchalant pose)*. I din't see nothin'.

(RINGMASTER's "Do it," NEW KID's action, BUL-LIED's cowering response and BYSTANDER's "I din't see nothin'" repeat until all but the last pair have been affected. With fewer than six actors, CLOWNS can simply keep switching positions for the desired number of interactions. Bullying routines may be repeats of tableaux above or new situations developed by cast. After each "I din't see nothin'," NEW KID gives a shout of joy, e.g., "What fun!" "What a rush!" "What a giggle!" "What a hoot!" Finally, NEW KID reaches the last pair and approaches the last BULLIED.)

RINGMASTER *(cracks whip. OTHERS jump and stop short)*. Wait! *(Pulls NEW KID over to last BYSTANDER.)* Do it to this one.
NEW KID. But this one didn't *choose* to—

RINGMASTER *(cracks whip. OTHERS jump)*. Do it!

(NEW KID bullies CLOWN AS LAST BYSTANDER. The foggy area between clowning and cruelty is entered and crossed in the upcoming interactions.)

CLOWN AS LAST BYSTANDER *(cowering)*. Hey! That hurt!
CLOWN AS LAST BULLIED *(maintaining cowered pose)*. Whoa! You don't say!

(Business repeats down the line, or, with fewer actors, with CLOWNS switching positions: RINGMASTER cracks whip; OTHERS jump; RINGMASTER points to each of the remaining CLOWNS AS BYSTANDERS in turn and commands, "Do it to that one!" NEW KID complies, but with growing consternation rather than shouts of joy—"I don't think..." "Are you sure...?" "This doesn't seem..." With each assault, CLOWN AS BYSTANDER says, "Hey, that hurt!" and cowers. Each CLOWN AS BULLIED says, "Whoa! No kidding!" while holding cowering pose. This repeats until all except RINGMASTER and NEW KID are cowering. A beat. The atmosphere has obviously changed for the worse. No longer grinning, CLOWNS look at one another, at RINGMASTER, and finally at NEW KID.)

CLOWNS *(pointing at RINGMASTER)*. Do it to that one!

(NEW KID complies.)

RINGMASTER. Hey! That hurt!
CLOWNS. Whoa! No kidding! *(They spin around and point at NEW KID.)* Do it to that one!

NEW KID. Uh-oh.

(CIRCUS MUSIC. RINGMASTER and CLOWNS rush NEW KID who hightails it around the stage a time or two with OTHERS in pursuit. Suddenly NEW KID stops short and turns to face them, one arm extended, like a police officer stopping traffic. OTHERS pile into one another in surprise. MUSIC abruptly stops. During the following dialogue, NEW KID removes fright wig, nose and clown suit while OTHERS watch in amazement.)

NEW KID *(cont'd)*. Andrew! *(or Andrea)*

CLOWNS. Huh?

NEW KID. That's my name. Andrew. *(Andrea)*

RINGLEADER. So what's that supposed to mean?

NEW KID. That's for me to know and for you to find out. Well, actually, it's for me to find out, too. *(Beat; picks up backpack.)* Hey! That's a fourth choice!

RINGMASTER. There are only three choices! You want to be in the act, you've got three choices!

NEW KID. Maybe there's another act.

RINGMASTER. What? Where?

NEW KID. When I find out, I'll let you know. This was fun…until it wasn't. I'm moving on.

RINGMASTER *(pleading)*. New Kid!

NEW KID. Andrew. *(Andrea)*

CLOWN #1 *(in amazement)*. I've got a name.

CLOWN #2. So do I.

CLOWN #3. Me, too.

(RINGMASTER starts to back away as CLOWNS begin introducing themselves to one another, one name at a time. Some shake hands. Some slap each other on the

back. *Some even hug. NEW KID holds a hand out to RINGMASTER.)*

NEW KID. Andrew. *(Andrea)*
RINGMASTER *(hesitates, then—)*. I liked you better when you were New Kid.
NEW KID. How do you know?
RINGMASTER. I just know, okay? I just know.
NEW KID *(shrugs)*. That's a choice, too, I guess.
RINGMASTER. THERE ARE ONLY THREE CHOICES!

(With a farewell gesture to RINGMASTER, NEW KID joins CLOWNS in introductions, handshakes, hugs. CLOWNS are also taking off fright wigs, false noses and clown suits to reveal street clothes.)

RINGMASTER. Hey! Who's coming with me?

(No response. RINGMASTER cracks whip once, twice, three times. OTHERS are too busy chatting with one another to notice.)

RINGMASTER *(cont'd)*. Stupid bunch of clowns!

(RINGMASTER turns and exits. CIRCUS MUSIC plays. NEW KID and CLOWNS exit in various directions, chatting in a relaxed way, in small groups of two and three. LIGHTS fade. MUSIC fades.)

END OF PLAY

Bystander Blues

By Trish Lindberg

CHARACTERS

KATIE .... sensitive, intelligent girl, slightly overweight

JOHNNY .... most popular boy in school, a mean-spirited bully

SAMANTHA .... most popular girl in school, the queen of mean

ERIC .... bystander, has known Katie since kindergarten

JESSICA .... bystander, afraid to be labeled "unpopular" by Samantha

BOBBY .... bystander, used to be friends with Johnny, now tries to steer clear

RACHEL .... bystander, feels sorry for Katie, not confident enough to stand up for her

MATTIE .... bystander, feels guilty but not enough to do anything

BRANDY .... bystander, has some status in the school, but still unwilling to support Katie

KARLA .... bystander, shy, unwilling to draw attention to herself

This play may also be performed by a smaller five-person cast by keeping the characters of Katie, Johnny and Samantha the same and alternating the rest of the lines between two actors (bystanders) on either side of the action. The only exception is in the section where Samantha tries to belittle Katie in front of Jessica. The lines said by Jessica in the original version should all be said by the same actor.

Gender doesn't matter in the two bystanders in this smaller cast version. I'm sure the play could also be expanded, if more cast members were needed, by dividing up the lines of all but Katie, Johnny and Samantha and being sure that the same actor plays the Jessica part in the section mentioned earlier. I look forward to all sorts of creative variations.

SETTING AND TIME: Bare stage with props. The present.

WORDS TO PONDER: *Bystanders have tremendous power to stop bullying if they would intervene, get help, and support the target of the bullying. There are so many more young people who "see" bullying and do nothing than those who actually bully. Hopefully, this play will encourage those who see bullying behavior in action to stop tolerating it by doing and saying something. There is power in numbers. Bystanders need to step up and do their part to stop the needless scars that bullying leaves on young people every day in school.*

(The BYSTANDERS [BRANDY, JESSICA, RACHEL and KARLA R and ERIC, BOBBY and MATTIE L] are standing upstage of KATIE and SAMANTHA, with their backs to the audience on either side of KATIE and SAMANTHA, who are in the center. KATIE and SAMANTHA are in a tableau, facing front about to begin their lines. JOHNNY is slightly upstage of them L with his back to the audience. As each of the BYSTANDERS speaks, they turn around front to the audience. When JOHNNY enters the scene, he, too, turns to interact with SAMANTHA and KATIE.)

BRANDY *(turns front)*. What happened yesterday

ERIC *(turns front)*. Never should have happened.
JESSICA *(turns front)*. I should have
BOBBY *(turns front)*. Said something,
RACHEL *(turns front)*. Done something,
MATTIE *(turns front)*. Anything,
KARLA *(turns front)*. But I didn't.

(The BYSTANDERS observe as SAMANTHA and KATIE come to life and begin interacting. KATIE is obviously nervous around SAMANTHA, uneasy and untrusting. SAMANTHA sees KATIE as an easy target and immediately pounces.)

SAMANTHA. Hey, what's up Katie?
KATIE. Nothing much.
SAMANTHA. I heard that you and Johnny…
KATIE. No way, Samantha… Who told you that?

(She turns away as JOHNNY turns and joins in the conversation. KATIE is even more uncomfortable now. JOHNNY is the most popular boy in school, and KATIE is most definitely not in his crowd. He intimidates her and is known to be cruel. KATIE would rather be anywhere than in the hallway stuck between SAMANTHA and JOHNNY.)

JOHNNY. Hi, ladies. How we doing?
SAMANTHA *(flirting)*. Hi, Johnny.

(KATIE turns away, trying to leave. JOHNNY blocks her way.)

JOHNNY. What's up with you?
KATIE. What do you mean?

(He sidles up to KATIE, looking back at SAMANTHA, obviously making fun of KATIE. KATIE again tries to get away.)

JOHNNY. What's your problem?
KATIE. Nothing. *(She pushes past him, dropping her books.)*
JOHNNY. Whoa. Back off.

(KATIE bends down to pick up her books. SAMANTHA goes over to her and feigns that she cares, all the while glancing back at JOHNNY. It is obvious the two of them have it in for KATIE.)

SAMANTHA. Katie? *(Whispering.)* What's the matter with you?

(JOHNNY leans down close to KATIE and touches her shoulder, obviously to intimidate her, looking back at SAMANTHA and winking.)

JOHNNY. She's cold, Sammy. Cold as ice…freeeeezing.

(SAMANTHA and JOHNNY laugh.)

SAMANTHA. Come on, Katie. Lighten up!
KATIE *(sarcastically)*. Thanks, Sam.

(KATIE finishes picking up her books and stands up. SAMANTHA confronts her.)

SAMANTHA. What's the big deal?

(JOHNNY boxes her in between him and SAMANTHA.)

JOHNNY. Yeah, Katie, what's the big *(throws his arms out to indicate big, making fun of her size)* deal? Big...you get it... Big deal!

(JOHNNY laughs, flirting with SAMANTHA who joins in the fun. JOHNNY and SAMANTHA exit upstage and turn their backs. KATIE freezes front center, a humiliated look on her face. If she could disappear, she would gladly do so. As the BYSTANDERS speak, each takes a step downstage, closer to KATIE.)

BRANDY. I saw what happened,

ERIC. And it never should have happened.

JESSICA. I should have said something like,

BOBBY. "Hey, Katie, what's up? Let's get out of here."

RACHEL. Done something, like stepped in and told Johnny to stop it.

MATTIE. Anything might have helped. I could have

BRANDY. Changed the subject,

ERIC. Gotten her outta there,

JESSICA. But I didn't.

BOBBY. I could have been there for her,

KARLA. But I wasn't.

(At this last line, KATIE, JOHNNY and all BYSTANDERS, except JESSICA and SAMANTHA, turn their backs. SAMANTHA begins scene with JESSICA, who doesn't want to be mean to KATIE but can't manage to confront SAMANTHA about her behavior.)

SAMANTHA *(to JESSICA)*. Katie is so sensitive. She can't even take a joke.

JESSICA *(uncomfortable)*. Huh?

SAMANTHA *(laughing)*. She made such a fool out of herself. What was she thinking?

JESSICA *(trying to pretend she doesn't know, even though she does)*. Who?

SAMANTHA. Katie. *(Incredulously.)* Didn't you see her?

JESSICA *(dismissively)*. Sort of…

SAMANTHA. How could you miss it? I am seriously worried about that girl.

JESSICA *(trying to change the subject)*. Maybe she's having a bad day.

SAMANTHA. You think? *(She laughs meanly and turns upstage.)*

JESSICA. I did see what happened.

BRANDY *(turning front)*. So did I.

ERIC *(turning front)*. I should have told Johnny to cut it out.

RACHEL *(turning front)*. I should have told Mrs. Smith.

BOBBY *(turning front)*. She's great to talk to.

KARLA *(turning front)*. And always follows through when students need help.

MATTIE *(turning front)*. I should've been a better friend.

ERIC. But I wasn't.

BRANDY. And I should've.

BOBBY. I know I could've.

RACHEL. But I didn't

ALL. Do anything. *(They all turn with their backs to the audience except KATIE.)*

KATIE *(turning front)*. It didn't end at school.

BRANDY *(turning front)*. When Katie got home I heard

ERIC *(turning front)*. Johnny had posted something about her on *facebook*.

RACHEL *(turning front)*. He just couldn't leave it alone.

KATIE. I was so humiliated.

BOBBY *(turning front)*. Everybody was talking about it.

SAMANTHA *(turning front and laughing)*. I thought Johnny's post was a riot.

KARLA *(turning front)*. I thought it was cruel.

KATIE. I didn't want to get out of bed, let alone go to school.

JOHNNY *(turning front and pointing at KATIE)*. She asked for it. What a jerk!

JESSICA *(turning front)*. She did nothing.

RACHEL. Neither did we.

BOBBY. And we should have,

ERIC. Could have,

KARLA. Done something,

BRANDY. Anything,

JESSICA. But we didn't.

BOBBY. We just walked away.

(ALL walk away except KATIE.)

RACHEL. Went on with our lives,

(ALL strike a pose in a tableau showing how they are going on with their lives.)

ERIC *(breaks pose to talk to audience)*. Pretended it wasn't happening,

KARLA *(breaks pose)*. Were glad it didn't happen to us,

MATTIE *(breaks pose)*. And steered clear.

BRANDY *(breaks pose)*. The next day Katie didn't come to school.

KATIE. I couldn't face them.

JESSICA *(breaks pose)*. A lot of kids,

BOBBY *(breaks pose)*. Pressured by Samantha,

RACHEL *(breaks pose)*. Wrote on Johnny's wall.

KARLA. I couldn't believe what they said.

KATIE. I felt so alone.

MATTIE. I felt so ashamed.

BRANDY. I felt so sad.

ERIC. I felt worried.

SAMANTHA. Johnny is so popular.

JESSICA. Samantha can be a witch if you get on her bad side.

KATIE. I didn't understand why.

BOBBY. I didn't understand how.

KARLA. I didn't understand at all.

BRANDY. Most of the kids liked me. I should have taken the time

RACHEL. To talk to her,

ERIC. To sit with her,

JESSICA. To be with her…

KATIE. I felt so alone.

MATTIE. No one did anything to help.

BOBBY. No one.

KARLA. Samantha and Johnny kept posting such evil things.

ERIC. Some of their *facebook* friends joined in the fun,

JOHNNY. Until it was completely out of control… *(He laughs meanly.)*

RACHEL. Really mean stuff like

JESSICA. You wouldn't believe

ERIC. How cruel.

MATTIE. You can just imagine.

KATIE *(increasingly desperate)*. I felt so alone.

KARLA. It went on and on.

BOBBY. No one, I mean no one

BRANDY. Did anything.

RACHEL. Why didn't I text her?

JESSICA. Why didn't I call her?

MATTIE. Why didn't I?

ALL BYSTANDERS. Why?

JOHNNY. She was so uptight.

KARLA. She was so alone.

SAMANTHA *(meanly)*. She was soooo sensitive!

BRANDY *(kindly)*. She was so sensitive.

BOBBY. No one did anything,

MATTIE. And everyone knew.

JESSICA. Johnny's *facebook* page

KARLA. I admit I looked at it.

MATTIE. I did too.

ERIC. I couldn't believe it!

BOBBY. Katie's not that fat.

KATIE *(imploringly)*. I was desperate.

MATTIE. Why didn't I do something?

JESSICA. Why didn't I tell someone?

RACHEL. Why didn't I help her?

BOBBY. Why didn't I?

ALL *(except KATIE)*. Why?

(ALL turn their backs on KATIE.)

KATIE. It would have made all the difference.

END OF PLAY

The Conundrum

By Brett Neveu

CHARACTERS

KEN...a 20-year-old
TONY ....a 14-year-old

SETTING AND TIME: Bare stage with props. The present.

(LIGHTS up on KEN and TONY. KEN wears slacks and a button-up shirt. He is rather tall. TONY wears gym clothes and dribbles a basketball. He is rather short.)

KEN *(to audience)*. Here's what happened:

TONY *(angry, to KEN)*. What're you scared or somethin', shrimp?

KEN. And that is where the conundrum began.

TONY. What conundrum?

KEN *(to TONY)*. You calling me a shrimp.

TONY. How's that a conundrum?

KEN. First off, I'm taller than you.

TONY. I wasn't referring to height when I called you a shrimp.

KEN. "Shrimp" always refers to height in this context. Gym class. Basketball. "Shrimp." Me, tall. You, short.

TONY. I was referring to your entire state of your whatever when I called you a shrimp.

KEN. My state of whatever?

TONY. Yeah. Your shrimpy actions. Your shrimpy body language. Your shrimpy everything.

KEN. You mind if I give this whole thing some context?

TONY. If you feel like you should so you can explain your stupid self, then go for it.

KEN *(to audience)*. This is the context. Tony Baker. Six years ago. Eighth grade. In gym class. Basketball. He'd been hassling me for months, with gems like:

TONY. Hey dog face.

KEN. And:

TONY. I hear you eat puke.

KEN. And my fave:

TONY. Look at me one more time and I'll punch your guts out your butt.

KEN. Out my *butt*.

TONY. And I'll do it, too.

KEN *(to TONY)*. You're fourteen. You can't punch that hard.

TONY. Try me and see.

KEN *(to audience)*. And right there, *that* was the problem. "Try me and see." In my mind, no matter what, I always imagined the consequences of what Tony might do to me.

TONY *(angry, to KEN)*. What're you scared or somethin', shrimp?

KEN. That was the one that got me thinking, though. Him saying that. The "shrimpy" thing. And, now, at age twenty, I still think about it. I think:

TONY. "What exactly could have happened if I had questioned the ridiculousness of the statement?"

KEN *(to TONY)*. Right.

TONY. But you understood the consequences.

KEN. Did I?

TONY. Gut punching.

KEN. But I'd never even see you even hit anybody. Ever.

TONY. But I might. You never know.

KEN. So you hit me. Then what?

TONY. I'd probably have gotten into big trouble.

KEN. And you would have blamed me for the trouble.

TONY. And then, later, you would have gotten punched even harder.

KEN. And then the same thing would have happened on and on and on, again and again, until each punch got worse and worse until I was one, big, fist-marked bruise. *(A pause.)*

TONY. You've got an active imagination.

KEN. So what.

TONY. I'm saying your description seems a little extreme.

KEN *(to the audience)*. Back to my *conundrum*.

TONY. Your conundrum.

KEN. The *consequences* of me calling Tony out, right there in gym class, about the whole "shrimp" thing. Of course, being the age I am now, I see all the alleys I could have taken. I could have said *(to TONY)* I'm taller than you.

TONY. You said that already.

KEN. No I didn't.

TONY. Yes you did.

KEN. Anyhow. Something else I could have said to him would have been…

TONY. Harder than you thought, isn't it?

KEN. No.

TONY. Then what else would you have said?

KEN. How about, "Nice shoes."

TONY. "Nice shoes"?

KEN. Yeah. Those gym shoes you had were pretty scuffed up.

TONY. "Nice shoes" has no affect on me whatsoever.

KEN. Okay. Well. Maybe it isn't about what I would have said, but more about me ignoring you and not being so frightened of what you might have done to me.

TONY. Fat chance.

KEN. "Fat chance"?

TONY. Like I said. You're a shrimp. In your mind. In your *soul*.

KEN. My soul is shrimpy?

TONY. Yeah.

KEN. Seriously?

TONY. Your soul is a total shrimp.

KEN *(to audience)*. This is what I paid attention to?

TONY. Six years' perspective really shines a light on my backwards logic, doesn't it.

KEN *(to TONY)*. It does.

TONY. So maybe start there.

KEN. Start where?

TONY. The consequences of your actions—

KEN. —and the *conundrum*.

TONY. The *conundrum*.

KEN. "What, in my mind, would have been the consequences of me standing up to you?" *(Pause.)* A punch in the gut.

TONY. A punch in the gut.

KEN. What else?

TONY. Humiliation?

KEN. Right! I would have been humiliated. In front of the whole class.

TONY. Why would you have been humiliated?

KEN. Because I would have said something really stupid.

TONY. You mean like calling somebody who is obviously much taller than you a "shrimp"?

KEN. Ah. Like you did. Point taken.

TONY. What if you would have said something short and to the point?

KEN. Like?

TONY. How about, "Grow up"?

KEN. Wow. Would that have worked?

TONY. Maybe.

KEN. Let's find out.

TONY. Okay. *(Angry, to KEN.)* What're you scared or somethin', shrimp?

KEN. "Grow up."

TONY. *You* grow up. *(A pause.)*

KEN. Hm.

TONY. I gave you quite a retort, didn't I?

KEN. Not really.

TONY. I'm making a point.

KEN. Which is?

TONY. It's not like I'm full of fancy comebacks or witticisms, either. I'm fourteen. Same as you.

KEN. So your mind and my mind worked similarly back then.

TONY. I wouldn't go that far.

KEN. I mean, neither one of us had any sort of snappy things to say to each other.

TONY. Right.

KEN. So what was your reason for taunting me in the first place?

TONY. Probably the same reason you didn't have anything snappy to say back to me.

KEN. Fear of getting punched?

TONY. Maybe not that one.

KEN. Fear of humiliation?

TONY. Possibly.

KEN. Because you were playing basketball in gym class. And you were short.

TONY. Maybe.

KEN. So you tried to take the attention off of that by taunting me.

TONY. That's fair.

KEN. But what was the purpose of all the other times you hassled me, outside of gym class?

TONY. You were tall. I was short. You were sensitive. I was pushy. You were in my gym class. I was in yours. Oil and water, buddy. Oil and water. They really just *don't mix.*

KEN. So my conundrum.

TONY. Your conundrum.

KEN. Isn't really a conundrum.

KEN. Six years of wondering about this.

TONY. Six years.

KEN. I wish I could go back in time—

TONY. You want to be fourteen again and fix the situation?

KEN. No. That wouldn't be me going back in time. That would be me being fourteen again. That's age regression. Not the same thing.

TONY. Oh.

KEN. If I could go back in time, I would find myself and tell myself, "Hey. You were called 'shrimp.' It made no sense, which makes total sense."

TONY. Because I was fourteen.

KEN. And my non-reaction? My lack of a snappy come-back?

TONY. You were fourteen.

KEN. And you probably weren't going to punch me.

TONY. But you thought I might.

KEN. Which was probably just as bad, the "fear of the punch."

TONY. Either way—

KEN. It's not a conundrum anymore.

(TONY dribbles the basketball.)

TONY *(angry, to KEN)*. What're you scared or somethin', shrimp?

KEN. Nope, I'm not.

TONY. What did you say, dog face?

KEN. I said, "Nope, I'm not."

TONY. I hear you eat puke.

KEN. I don't eat puke.

TONY. I'm gonna punch you until your guts fall out your butt.

KEN. Impossible. *(A pause.)*

TONY. Fine.

KEN *(smiling)*. Fine.

(LIGHTS fade to black.)

END OF PLAY

Downhill

By Eric Coble

CHARACTERS

CYNTHIA ..... a woman with employee problems, 30s to 40s
MICHAEL .... a man with boss problems, 40s
JACOB .... a teenager with parent problems, 17
TRAVIS .... a teenager with teenage problems, 16
EMMA .... a younger girl with markers

SETTING AND TIME: An office, a home, a school, another home. Now.

PRODUCTION NOTES: *Downhill* can be performed by actors of any gender or ethnicity. The names are a guideline, not a requirement: for example, Cynthia can be changed to a man or Jacob to a woman. Sets should be simple or non-existent for maximum speed and flow between scenes.

(CYNTHIA, in sharp business dress, faces off with MICHAEL, in a shirt and tie, holding file folders. They are in CYNTHIA's office.)

CYNTHIA. One simple thing.
MICHAEL. I know.
CYNTHIA. I gave you one simple thing to do, Michael.
MICHAEL. And I was mostly successful—
CYNTHIA. And Lewis and Franklin Dwadzik were mostly successful in creating an airplane in 1894. Except that

their machine crashed and killed them both in a horrible mass of broken metal. You know who *did* succeed? The Wright Brothers. Which ones do we talk about today?

MICHAEL. The Wright Brothers.

CYNTHIA. The Wright Brothers. Not the Dwadzik Brothers. The Wright Brothers.

MICHAEL. Do the Dwadzik Brothers even really exist?

CYNTHIA. They did! Before they died as horrible failures! Are you trying to take this company down with the Dwadziks, Michael?

MICHAEL. No, ma'am.

CYNTHIA. Then why did you screw up?

MICHAEL. I didn't screw up, we're on our way to making it work, just two more days—

CYNTHIA. Which I did not give you.

MICHAEL. —which you did not give us—

CYNTHIA. You know why I didn't give you those two more days?

MICHAEL. Because—

CYNTHIA. Because I see the big picture, Michael. It is my job to keep the big picture in my mind at all times, Michael. It is your job to do what I tell you to do, Michael. Is that so hard?

MICHAEL. No, ma'am.

CYNTHIA. Is that beyond your capabilities?

MICHAEL. No, ma'am.

CYNTHIA. Are you a Dwadzik?

MICHAEL. No, ma'am.

CYNTHIA. Then why do you keep screwing up?!

MICHAEL. I'm trying. We're all trying—

CYNTHIA. Dwadzik.

MICHAEL. Oh, come on—

CYNTHIA *(in his face)*. Dwadzik, Dwadzik, Dwadzik.

MICHAEL. This is not—

CYNTHIA. Dwadzik! *(MICHAEL glares at her, silently.)* Breathe in. What do you smell?

MICHAEL. …nothing.

CYNTHIA. Exactly. There are no stinking piles of fail in my office. However, every time I walk past your cubicle, there is the undeniable stench of fresh fail reeking from your chair, your desk, your shoes. I did not start this company so you could track your mess in here every time you slouch through my door. So unless you want to go on sitting in your stinking pile of failure—which you can do on your own time, that can be arranged—I suggest you take a success shower, wash your clothes in high-heat success detergent, and show up ready to work for once! Do I make myself clear?

MICHAEL. Completely.

(CYNTHIA exits. MICHAEL turns, slams down his file folders as JACOB walks in, texting. They are at home.)

JACOB. Hey, Dad.

(MICHAEL nods. JACOB sits and texts.)

MICHAEL. Have you finished your homework?

JACOB. Most of it.

MICHAEL. Then off with the phone. You know the rules.

JACOB *(texting)*. I just gotta finish checking with Brian about the party.

MICHAEL. No. Homework now.

JACOB. In a minute—

MICHAEL *(grabbing the phone)*. Now, Jacob!

JACOB. Hey!

MICHAEL. One simple thing! I ask you to do one simple thing!

JACOB. I know—

MICHAEL. Are you keeping up with your math?

JACOB. I'm pretty good, can I—

MICHAEL. No, not pretty good. You know who was pretty good? Your grandfather, who dropped out of school and had three kids to support, going door to door to door with his junk used Hoover vacuum cleaners. I did not get where I am today so you could end up like him and the Dwadzik Brothers!

JACOB. Who?

MICHAEL. Is school somehow beyond your brain's abilities?

JACOB. No.

MICHAEL. Are you your grandfather and his Hoovers?

JACOB. No!

MICHAEL. Then why do you keep screwing up?

JACOB. I don't! I try!

MICHAEL. Hoover.

JACOB. I'm doing my best—

MICHAEL *(in his face)*. Hoover Hoover Hoover.

JACOB. You're not even—

MICHAEL. Hoover! *(JACOB glares at him.)* You want to be a screw-up, you do it on your own time, you get a job, your own house, your own food and clothes. As long as you are under my roof, you will not sit there in a big stinking pile of fail, crying "I tried" "I tried" "I tried," do you understand me?

JACOB. Yes, sir.

MICHAEL. Then get to work!

(MICHAEL storms off as JACOB turns to TRAVIS, a slightly smaller kid than JACOB, carrying a backpack. They are in a school hallway. TRAVIS sees JACOB, turns to walk away.)

JACOB *(calls out)*. Yo, Travis.

TRAVIS. …hey, Jake. *(He walks away.)*

JACOB. Where you goin', man?

TRAVIS. I gotta get to class.

JACOB. You're goin' the long way.

TRAVIS. Am I?

JACOB. You get the geometry?

TRAVIS. I was gonna finish it in class— I haven't—

JACOB. *I* need to finish it in class. You were supposed to do it last night and get it to me.

TRAVIS. I got busy—

JACOB. One thing, Travis. I asked you for one simple thing.

(TRAVIS tries to get past him, JACOB blocks his way.)

TRAVIS. I know.

JACOB. Do you want me to fail?

TRAVIS. No, I told you, I got too busy—

JACOB. Too busy? You know who got too busy? I might get too busy to tell my fists not to jack you up after school.

TRAVIS. You have to verbally tell your fists what to do?

JACOB *(shoves him)*. Are you getting smart?

TRAVIS. No.

JACOB. You want my fists to get busy?

TRAVIS. No.

JACOB *(fists in his face)*. Jack! Jack! Jack!

TRAVIS. Don't—

JACOB. Jack! *(TRAVIS stands, scared.)* I have a lot—a lot riding on this year. I did not get this far just to watch it all go down the toilet because some stupid geek punk who gets everything easy won't take the time to share one stupid piece of paper every morning. Do you get it?

TRAVIS I get it.

(TRAVIS hands the sheet to JACOB who walks away. TRAVIS turns as EMMA, his younger sister, enters, spreads paper all over the floor and flops down coloring. They are at home.)

EMMA. Hi, Travis. *(TRAVIS grunts, throwing down his backpack.)* Do you want to color with me?

TRAVIS. I don't have time.

EMMA. Please? Just one picture?

TRAVIS. Will you please move your papers? They're all over the place; this is my house too.

EMMA. I was just coloring.

TRAVIS. I've asked you to please just pick up after yourself—is that so hard?

EMMA. No.

TRAVIS One simple thing, Emma…that's all… I… *(He looks at her. She watches him. He lets out a breath.)* I'm sorry. I just need to do my homework and I feel like I'm always picking up after you.

EMMA. I'm trying.

TRAVIS. I know you are.

EMMA. One picture?

TRAVIS. I'll color one picture with you and then it's time to clean up, okay?

EMMA. Okay. Will you help me?

TRAVIS *(sits)*. Don't you know where your stuff goes by now?

EMMA. I do, I just like when you help me. I could help you then. I could sharpen your pencil.

TRAVIS *(slight smile)*. Deal. What should we color?

EMMA. How about a picture…of you and me holding hands. Walking.

TRAVIS. I can do that. *(Nods, coloring.)* I can do that.

(BLACKOUT.)

END OF PLAY

The Final Testimony
of Henry Samson

By Y York

CHARACTERS

PETER......age 16, male, attentive, smart, apologetic up to a point
HENRY SAMSON......................age 16, male, charming, cunning
ALICE .... age 16, female, attractive, sweet, happy, self-effacing
THE KID IN AN EXPENSIVE SUIT .... age 16, male,
slick and scary

SETTING AND TIME: A courtroom. The present.

NOTE: "…" is a breath, a thought, a very short amount of time passes, but a shift has happened. "—" is an interrupted line, usually by the next speaker but sometimes by the current speaker.

(An almost empty courtroom. PETER, sports jacket and tie, looks over his documents. ALICE, dressed in a lovely dress, is sitting in the gallery near THE KID IN AN EXPENSIVE SUIT. Enter HENRY SAMSON, dressed nicely but casually, no tie or jacket. He swaggers, is amazed and confused but not worried.)

PETER. Hello, Henry. Glad you could finally join us. We've been waiting for you.
HENRY. You've been waiting for me?
PETER. Yes, we need to hear your side of things—

HENRY. My side of what?

PETER. We're just trying to get to the bottom of—

HENRY. Is this about my dad's car—? Because I wasn't drinking—

PETER. Oh no, it's not about the crash—the crash is settled.

HENRY. Oh. *(Calming down.)* Okay. Who are you?

PETER. Oh, my bad. I'm Peter. *(Handshake.)* How do you do?

HENRY. Fine. *(Whisper.)* Why the tie, friend?

PETER. I beg your pardon?

HENRY. Really. Your mom make you wear that?

PETER. I want to show respect—

HENRY. Yeah, I know. I leave it on until I'm out the door, and then stick it in my pocket. She never finds out.

PETER. I want to show respect for the court.

HENRY *(looking around)*. Yeah, wow, a court. What's this about, Pete?

PETER. Peter. It's about July 4th.

HENRY. What, the Declaration of Independence?

PETER. Ha—good one. No. Last July 4th.

HENRY. ...Last July 4th... That's a long time ago. Last summer. I don't remember.

(THE KID stands, points steadily at HENRY. HENRY sees him.)

PETER. I know, I'm sorry. This system is archaic, there ought to be some way we could...but there isn't, and there's nothing I can do about it, we couldn't start until now. Can we just go over a few things—? And then you can go.

HENRY. What's he doing—?

PETER *(to KID)*. Will you please sit down? *(KID sits, stops pointing.)*

HENRY *(to KID)*. Yeah, no loaded fingers allowed in the courtroom, buddy. *(Recognizes ALICE. To PETER.)* Is that...? What's Alice doing here? I thought she moved away.

PETER. She did. But now she's here. Because she was there.

ALICE *(waving)*. Hi, Henry.

HENRY. Hey, Alice. *(To PETER.)* I thought she moved. She's a nice girl, but, you know, a little...you know.

PETER. I don't think I do know.

HENRY. You know. On the outside looking in?

PETER. ...We should get started.

HENRY. Okay, let's do this. How can I help you?

PETER. Let's start with what happened.

HENRY. Okay, but I already said I don't remember—

(THE KID stands and points steadily at HENRY.)

PETER. Do you, Henry Samson, swear and promise to tell the truth?

HENRY. What's with the pointing, Mister Finger Man?! Who is that guy?

PETER. He's always here— *(To and for THE KID.)* Can't get rid of him to save my life. *(THE KID sits. To HENRY.)* Just say, "I swear and promise to tell the truth."

HENRY. I swear and promise to tell the truth.

PETER *(chuckling apologetically)*. So help me God.

HENRY. Whoa.

PETER. Please...

HENRY. So help me God.

PETER. Great. You can sit down. *(HENRY heads to the witness stand.)* No, not there. Not yet. *(Points to gallery.)* Over there. Alice?

(HENRY crosses to the gallery as ALICE heads for the witness stand. They pass each other.)

HENRY *(with bravado).* Hi, Alice. Long time no see. Sure could use you back in math class. You look nice. Nice dress.

ALICE. Thanks. I really like it, too.

HENRY *(whisper).* Do you know what any of this is about?

ALICE *(yes).* Uh-huh.

HENRY. Who's the Suit?

ALICE. I don't know, but he's very quiet.

PETER. Henry, please sit. Alice. *(Gestures to the witness stand.)*

(ALICE sits in the witness seat; HENRY sits in the gallery, as far as possible from THE KID.)

PETER. Alice, you've already been sworn. Would you please tell us what happened last July 4th?

ALICE. Okay. It was before the fireworks, I was just standing around... I didn't think Henry liked me or anything. Boys like pretty girls, not chubby ones, and I know that, but he was nice, so I—

HENRY. I bought you a hot dog. Remember that? I bought her a hot dog.

ALICE. Yeah, it was good, thanks.

PETER. Go on, Alice.

ALICE. He said he knew a really cool place to watch the fireworks, near the mud flats, closer to the lake, away from the noisy crowd. We went down through the trees and grass, and I had on high heels—I was trying to look nice, but they really hurt, and it was really muddy—

HENRY. Of course it was muddy, it was the mud flats.

ALICE. Ha—. Good one.

(PETER and ALICE laugh at HENRY's joke; THE KID does not. HENRY puffs up.)

PETER. Go on, Alice.

ALICE. He kissed me. It was really sweet, on the cheek. Then it was different. A grownup kiss.

PETER. Did you like it?

ALICE. I did, it was…it was exciting, but it was too grown-up, and we were far away, and it was dark. And it was muddy—I was getting all muddy—

HENRY *(standing)*. Just a minute, here—

PETER. You will get your chance—

HENRY. You're getting a distorted picture—you should have let me talk first—

(THE KID is now behind HENRY. With just a light finger touch on HENRY's head, he pushes HENRY into his seat. IIENRY is surprised at the force of it.)

HENRY *(sitting down)*. Okay, okay.

PETER. Please, go on, Alice.

ALICE. He said, "I can tell you like it, come on, let's have some fun." He leaned back and he wanted me to…you know…the thing with the thing? But I didn't want to.

HENRY. Why would I do that? I can get any girl I want.

PETER. Can we please have order in the court?

HENRY. This is ridiculous, and don't you touch me with that finger, I'm the victim here, you heard her say I was nice. I didn't make her do anything.

PETER. We'll hear your testimony after we hear from Alice.

ALICE. Ladies first, Henry.

PETER. Go on, Alice.

ALICE. He said—he said that I might as well do it, because everybody saw us go down to the lake together, so everybody was going to think so already, and it was just the thing with the thing, and maybe I'd like it.

HENRY. No no no no.

(THE KID sits next to HENRY, shows HENRY his finger. HENRY is quiet.)

PETER. So you did it.

ALICE. Yeah, I did it. I *didn't* like it. But I did it.

PETER. What happened after that?

ALICE. He left me there. I didn't see him again that night.

PETER. So that was the end of it?

ALICE. Sort of. I tried to forget. It was summer, so I didn't have to see him in school or anything. But when football practice started *(brief pause)* he told all the players. He told everybody. He told them I asked, I asked to do it. A friend of mine told me… Henry said I asked.

PETER. How did that make you feel?

ALICE. I was…I felt…humiliated.

PETER. And now?

ALICE. Oh, no, I'm fine now. I love my dress.

PETER. It's beautiful.

ALICE. It never gets dirty. I got to pick it out.

PETER. Okay, Alice, thanks a lot. You're done.

(PETER immediately turns to HENRY. ALICE quietly leaves the court, while HENRY and PETER engage.)

PETER. Comments?

HENRY. You bet I have comments. I'm not going to let that go un…un…unrefutiated *(sic)*.

PETER. You want to take the stand?

HENRY. Yes, I do. *(To THE KID.)* You…just stay here, Finger Man. *(He hurries to the witness seat.)* That's not what happened, I mean, some of it happened, but not like that, I mean, come on, look at me, look at me.

PETER. Remember, you promised to tell the truth.

HENRY. Yes, and I am.

PETER. And you are allowed to include an apology.

HENRY. An apology—? No. I am going to clarify—let's have a clarification here…I can always get a girl, they fall all over me. But that's not even the point, I have a girl-friend, and me and her, well, we're pretty serious, and we don't, you know, cheat.

PETER. So, you're saying you weren't at the lake on July 4th?

HENRY. No, I was there. I don't really like the Fourth of July, all the noise and the smoke, but you can't avoid it so I thought I might as well go to the lake, and besides, I was lonely, my girlfriend was away, so I went to the lake for the fireworks, and I see Alice, and I know her because we have algebra together, and she's smart in algebra and I admire that. So I say, "Hi, how're you doing, let's get a hotdog and celebrate America's birthday together." So I get her a hotdog, and everything is cool…and then she says…she says about how…her ears, her ears are all sensitive, and she wants to see the fireworks and all, but she's worried about her ears. *(THE KID stands and points at HENRY, then crooks his finger in a come-hither fashion.)* Stop it, stop it, will you please—is that even legal, a finger like that in a courtroom?

PETER *(to THE KID)*. Please? *(THE KID stops pointing but stays standing. To HENRY.)* Go ahead, Henry.

HENRY. Alice wanted to go down to the lake to get away from the noise, but she didn't want to go by herself. So, I'm a gentleman, I offer to…escort her. I *escort* her down to the lake, and we sit down…and…and she asks me. She asks. She *asks*! And I…I don't want to, but I don't want her to feel bad. Imagine how bad she'd feel if I turn her down? So I let her. I let her even though it means I'm cheating on my girlfriend, that's how much I don't want Alice to feel bad. And that other business, telling the football team? Why would I do that? That's not something to brag about. Alice, who would brag about her?

(A moment of silence. PETER is sad. THE KID folds his arms in triumph.)

HENRY *(contd)*. Really. That's the truth. *(Brief pause.)* Say something.

PETER. We already know the truth. *(Last chance.)* Is there anything else you want to say? Something you want to say to Alice?

HENRY. That was the whole truth. That's how I remember it.

PETER. …"Throw the dog a bone"?

HENRY. What?

PETER. "Throw the dog a bone." Do you remember saying that phrase to the football team? *(Silence.)* I see you do remember.

HENRY. …I was…I was…

PETER. That's enough. We've heard enough. *(To THE KID.)* Take him.

HENRY. Take me where? *(Scared now.)* I don't want to go with him. It wasn't that big a deal. She's fine now, she said she's fine. Ask her, ask her… Where did she go?

PETER. She's gone. She was only here to testify.

HENRY. Call her, call her up. Where does she live?

PETER. She doesn't live. She killed herself after you told everybody your version of you and Alice at the lake.

HENRY. I thought they moved away.

PETER. They moved away. And she killed herself.

HENRY. I hardly remember July 4th. It wasn't that big a deal.

PETER. Well, this is.

HENRY. I want to call my dad.

PETER. Your dad is at your funeral. But don't worry, he's not mad about the car. Or the drinking.

HENRY. Don't I get a chance to say something?

PETER. You did. And you did. *(To THE KID.)* He's all yours.

(THE KID spreads his fingers wide, holds his palm vertically, HENRY is pulled to it like metal to magnet.)

END OF PLAY

Flash Mob

By Elizabeth Wong

CHARACTERS

ISABELLE "IZZIE" PEN .... 16, sweet, bright, athletic;
         sporting a bouncy ponytail, dressed in tennis whites;
         an up-and-comer on her high-school tennis team
DEENA SAVAGE .... 16, Izzie's tormentor and arch
         nemesis; best player on the team
MIKE CHAMPION ....17, captain of the football team
         and quintessential All-American boy
WEBMASTER..Internet gatekeeper;
         an intimidating sentry
FACETIME CHORUS (3m) or (2m, 1w)..........energetically
         recreates a fun social networking website
INSTANT MESSAGE "I.M." CHORUS (3w)......... Deena's
         friends, also on tennis team: KRISTI and JESSICA,16,
         and NICOLE, 15, Izzie's former friend
STUDENTS.....football team, cheer/pep squad, student body
         council, drill/flag team, marching band, math/drama clubs

SETTING AND TIME: A social networking website. The present.

PLAYWRIGHT'S NOTE: As you may have guessed, the title suggests a possible course of action beyond the play. An activism inspired by "Pink Shirt Day," organized by two 12th-graders in Nova Scotia after bullies picked on a 9th-grade boy for wearing a pink shirt to his first day of school. Thanks to the reach of the World Wide Web, this anti-bullying event went global, with participants world-wide wearing pink in solidarity. Peer pressure gone positive, *and public.*

ACKNOWLEDGMENTS: Many thanks to the Sergel family, Dramatic Publishing Company, and Linda Habjan, the mastermind behind the bully project, for this marvelous opportunity to do something useful. Also, many thanks to Christine Dominick; Char Borman; Doug Cooney, my Bully Play buddy; Sandra Weintraub, my sounding board; and a special shout-out to my brother and my middle nephew for their insight and invaluable suggestions.

(In the dark, SOUND of an Apple computer booting up, then LIGHTS up on sentry-like WEBMASTER who blocks the way, and on IZZIE who holds a broken tennis racket.)

WEBMASTER. Log on!
IZZIE. Izzie, two zees, two eyes, no y.
WEBMASTER. Password! *(IZZIE whispers a password into his ear.)* Connecting. Welcome to FaceTime!

(A FACETIME CHORUS recreates a social networking website with a dizzying array of overlapping options.)

FACETIME #1. Your mother wants to be your friend. Accept. Reject. *(IZZIE reacts with consternation.)*
FACETIME #2. Farmer Fred. Café Life. Bedazzled. Yard Monster. Mafia Mobsters.
FACETIME #3. Pinky Nishiwara just answered questions about Isabelle. Do you think Isabelle will ever be kissed? Yes? No? See what they said.

FACETIME #1. Honey, I know it's not cool to friend your mom.

FACETIME #2. Happy Fishtank. Draw My Stuff. Zombie Attack. Bubble Paradise!

FACETIME #3. Trevor Wells found some white mystery eggs. He's excited to hatch a rare chicken and wants to share. Comment. Hatch an egg.

FACETIME #2. You, Arlene Morrissey, and nine hundred and fifty-three thousand others *like Wizards of Waverly Place*. Unlike? Comment?

FACETIME #3. What's on your mind? What's on your mind? What. Is. On. Your…

IZZIE. I'll tell you what is on my mind. A certain "star player" hid my tennis racket, *again*! Half the team was in on it. That evil witch just sat back, watched me run around the locker room like a complete idiot. I don't get why she's so mean to me. I've never done anything to her. Nothing. So yes, finally, I told. They say if you are being bullied, tell someone. Tell an adult. So I did. I told coach. I said, coach, this certain *person* bullies me on a daily basis. Just now, I saw her take some scissors and put something behind the AV equipment. This is what I found. *(She holds up her damaged racket.)* My mom and dad are gonna explode when they have to restring my racket, again! Two years I've put up with this kind of abuse. I'll go to the bathroom; when I come back, my racket is gone. My books, my backpack scattered all over the classroom. I'm sick of it. The insults. The putdowns. That's what I told coach. You'd think the number-one player would have more class, but Deena Savage is crazy schizo. Coach says, "Sorry Izzie, I haven't noticed anything, but I'll keep an eye on it. I'll take this up with the girls' dean." *(Sigh.)* I don't know what to expect, but maybe, finally, hopefully, things are gonna get better.

(CHIME of an instant message. An INSTANT MESSAGE CHORUS enter. They are KRISTI, JESSICA and NICOLE—IZZIE's teammates in tennis whites. Special LIGHT on IZZIE's bully and star player, DEENA SAVAGE, who orchestrates her friends even from afar with a wink, nudge, gesture or simple look.)

INSTANT MESSAGE #1 *(from KRISTI)*. Hey Itchy Bitchy, how does it feel to be a snitch!

INSTANT MESSAGE #2 *(from NICOLE)*. Snitch! Snitch! Izzie Snitchy!

INSTANT MESSAGE #3 *(from JESSICA)*. Find your tennis racket, snitch?

(JESSICA snatches the racket out of IZZIE's hand. ALL cackle with laughter.)

DEENA SAVAGE. Cat gut 60 pounds. L M A O [Netspeak: Laughing My Ass Off].

INSTANT MESSAGES #1, 2, 3 & DEENA. R O F L! [Rolling On the Floor Laughing]. R O F L!

IZZIE. You know what? I'm not going to dignify them with a reply. *(She turns away.)*

DEENA. Smiley, with a wink and a grin. *(She nudges KRISTI.)*

INSTANT MESSAGE #2 *(from KRISTI)*. Why R U making trouble for Deena? You snitched to Coach and the girls' dean. So not cool.

(The I.M. CHORUS close in on IZZIE.)

INSTANT MESSAGE #3 *(from JESSICA)*. Yeah, snitcher. Deena is state singles champ. You're just a pathetic loser.

INSTANT MESSAGE CHORUS (ALL). Loser!

IZZIE. O M G!!! [Oh My God!] Instead of one bully, now I got three more. Jessica, don't you realize we won the team trophy because I won my quarterfinals match? I am not a loser. *(JESSICA mouths the word "loser.")* Pathetic. Deena pulls your string; you puppets do her dirty work. You're a bunch of sheep. What did I ever do to you?

INSTANT MESSAGE #2 *(from NICOLE)*. Deena, why are we doing this to Izzie?

DEENA. No reason. Because I feel like it.

INSTANT MESSAGE #1 *(from KRISTI)*. I just don't like your face!

INSTANT MESSAGE #2 *(from NICOLE)*. Well, uh, I don't like your hair.

IZZIE. *Et tu*, Nicole, I thought we were friends. Since Brownies! So much for Girl Scout honor.

INSTANT MESSAGE #2 *(from NICOLE)*. Sorry Izzie, better you than me.

INSTANT MESSAGE #3 *(from JESSICA)*. Itchy Bitchy, we don't like your hair or your face. We just don't like *you*. No one likes you!

(LIGHTS up on a bystander, MIKE CHAMPION, in a football uniform, fresh from practice. He observes IZZIE, the mean girls from afar, and he's seen enough. The GIRLS pose cutesy to draw MIKE's attention; he ignores them. CHIME alert!)

MIKE. Hey, Isabelle, you there? Izzie? Don't let Deena and her posse get you down. They're not worth it. They got no class.

(The mean GIRLS, and DEENA, exit.)

IZZIE. Thanks, Mike. It's hard... *(holds back tears)* ... because everyone, it feels like everyone is against me.

MIKE. Not everyone is against you. Stupid is as stupid does.

IZZIE. Forrest Gump. I like that movie. Box of chocolates. L O L [Laughing Out Loud].

MIKE. Smiley with a grin. But seriously, you gotta stand up to them. Don't take what they're shoveling. Take charge.

IZZIE. I did that. But that's the problem. Standing up to them, I think I made things way worse. Especially after I told Coach Hurley, who told Mrs. Tyler, the girls' dean. Big mistake. Big, big mistake. Now Deena and her posse are really coming after me.

MIKE. That took a helluva lot of courage.

IZZIE. Mrs. Tyler calls me into her office, and I tell her about what Deena's been doing to me. Deena and her parents get called into her office. The dean shows them my racket, and Deena actually admits she's been tormenting me nonstop for the past two years. Mrs. Tyler told me Deena admitted she was bullying me.

MIKE. So, what's gonna happen to Deena? Is she getting suspended?

IZZIE. Nothing is happening to Deena. No suspension. No punishment. No apology, not even a slap on the wrist. NOTHING! Mrs. Tyler only told Deena to stay away from me, and to stop harassing me. That's it. I don't know what to do. I still have to see Deena and her evil minions in class, at practice, tournaments. What's worse, I feel everyone is blaming *me* for causing trouble for Deena, the *star* tennis player. *I'm* the victim, not her.

MIKE. Sorry, Izzie. Yeah, I heard the rumors. Sucks. The dean shoulda made Deena responsible for any retaliation from her friends.

IZZIE. Duh! She has a LOT of friends. Grownups are so clueless. Wait. B R B [Be Right Back]. Parent! *(ALL freeze a moment, then unfreeze.).* Sorry. P O S [Parent Over Shoulder].

MIKE. Smiley with tongue sticking out. *(Beat.)* Just hang tough.

IZZIE. So says THE most popular guy in school.

MIKE. True. Hey, I've got this assignment for AP Psych, maybe you could be my project. I could teach you to be intimidating. Don't smile, stare without blinking, and don't respond when spoken to; also helps to be six-feet four and 190 pounds wet.

IZZIE. L O L. I wish I could just sneak into Deena's bedroom and tattoo a big fat capital B on her forehead with a Sharpie, kinda like in…

MIKE. …*The Scarlet Letter.* Hawthorne. Don't remind me. AP Lit.

IZZIE. Mike. Lightbulb!!! I just got this crazy idea. But, uh, I need to borrow your popularity.

MIKE. You want to borrow my popularity? Sure. OK. Huh?

IZZIE. I'm sending you something.

FACETIME #1. Isabelle Pen sends you an event.

MIKE. Okay, clicking on it.

FACETIME #2. B 2 KUL 2 BULLY! ANTI-BULLYING RALLY! SHOW YOUR SUPPORT. WEAR YOUR SHADES TO SHOW UR 2 KUL TO BULLY! Will you attend? Comment. Yes, no, maybe. Remove?

MIKE. Brilliant, Izzie. Genius. I want in.

(Computer CHIMES, meaning "Yes I Will!")

IZZIE. Glad you feel that way, Mike. Because, uh, if you could…

MIKE. Done. It's gone global. I reposted under my name to everyone on my friends list and told them to spread the word.

FACETIME #2. B 2 KUL 2 BULLY! ANTI-BULLYING RALLY! SHOW YOUR SUPPORT. WEAR YOUR SHADES TO SHOW UR 2 KUL TO BULLY! Will you attend?

(Computer CHIMES, meaning "Yes I Will!")

FACETIME #3. Mike Champion and Isabelle Pen will attend the 2KUL2BULLY Anti-Bullying Rally. Will you attend?

(IZZIE and MIKE put on their cool shades.)

FACETIME #1. Mike Champion and the entire football team will attend the 2KUL2BULLY Anti-Bullying Rally. Will you attend?

(More CHIMES. The FOOTBALL TEAM joins. Simultaneously, they all take out their sunglasses, put them on all at once.)

FACETIME #2. The Student Body Council, the Pep and Cheer Squad, will all attend the 2KUL2BULLY Anti-Bullying Rally. Will you attend?

(STUDENTS enter and, as they take their places, put on their shades. "Yes, I will attend" CHIMES repeatedly.)

FACETIME #3. The Marching Band, the Drill Team, the Math and Drama Clubs, will all attend the 2KUL2 BULLY Anti-Bullying Rally.

(More STUDENTS enter, wearing sunglasses. Multiple CHIMES.)

FACETIME #1. Kristi, Jessica, Nicole and Deena will attend the 2KUL2BULLY Anti-Bullying Rally.

(KRISTI, JESSICA, NICOLE and DEENA enter, wearing sunglasses. CHIME SOUNDS.)

MIKE nudges IZZIE as DEENA and her minions join. More bespectacled STUDENTS also enter, some carry placards with letters on them.

They spell: D.E.E.N.A. B.E. N.I.C.E.

DEENA is horrified. She grabs placards spelling her name, rips them up. NICOLE, IZZIE's former friend, steps away from her old posse to videotape the event with a handheld video camera.)

NICOLE. Hey, Deena, yoo-hoo, smile for the camera. *(Waves her video camera.)* Can you say YouTube?!

(DEENA, cowed, pushes NICOLE out of the way, and exits with her posse, minus NICOLE, who now sidles up to IZZIE.)

IZZIE. What's up with you, Nicole?
NICOLE *(to IZZIE)*. Girl Scout honor.
IZZIE *(nods)*. Girl Scout honor.
FOOTBALL PLAYERS/EVERYONE ELSE *(in a call-and-response chant)*. We Are!/Too Cool! We Are!/Too Cool! We Are!/Too Cool!

(STUDENTS turn over cards that spell: 2.K.U.L.2. B.U.L.L.Y. N.O.T.K.U.L.2.B.U.L.L.Y.)

ALL *(cheer and clap)*. WOOT! WOOT!

(The FOOTBALL TEAM lifts IZZIE up for a victory parade upstage, IZZIE's arms raised overhead in triumph.

ALL freeze!

The FACETIME CHORUS and the WEBMASTER remain downstage.)

FACETIME #1. Two thousand and sixty-four people *viewed* the 2KUL2BULLY ANTI-BULLYING RALLY!

FACETIME #2. Six thousand five hundred and ninety-eight people nationwide *like* the 2KUL2BULLY ANTI-BULLYING RALLY!

FACETIME #3. One point two million people, and count-ing, *joined* the *International* 2KUL2BULLY ANTI-BULLYING RALLY!

WEBMASTER. Sleep? Restart? Shut down? Log off? *(Beat.)* Logging off.

(LIGHTS fade to black.)

END OF PLAY

Gasp, Farrah & Monster

By José Cruz González

CHARACTERS

YOUNG MAN .... teen, dressed in 1950s-style clothing,
uses an oxygen tank to catch his breath

YOUNG WOMAN...... teen, dressed in 1970s-style clothing,
has a Farrah Fawcett haircut

MONSTER .... teen, dressed in a dark suit and tie,
holds a briefcase

SETTING AND TIME: Anywhere and anytime.

WORDS TO PONDER: *"Cada persona es un mundo."*
(Each person is a separate reality.)

Gasp

(YOUNG MAN stands, holding an oxygen tank and breathing into a mask several times before speaking to us.)

YOUNG MAN. Railroads and rail cars. Can't get much better than that. I love the smell of diesel. Runnin' full speed with the wind at your face. It's my little piece of heaven.

(He gasps and breathes into the mask several times.)

131

A railroad cut across my backyard. At night I could hear the train rollin' by. It always called to me. "Get on board, sonny. Life's an adventure." My old man said I wouldn't amount to much. Made me grow up hard. When I wasn't workin' I was playin' on them tracks. It was my only playground helpin' me to escape the world I was trapped in. I'd imagine myself runnin' as fast I could and catchin' that train to some-where I don't know.

(He gasps and breathes into the mask several times.)

There was a fella at school I didn't much like. A momma's boy. He was smaller than me. I picked on him 'cause he dressed nice and carried a sack lunch his momma made him. Got to the point where he was so scared of me he would hide, but I would still seek him out. I remember that fear in his eyes when he'd see me comin'. I liked making people laugh at the expense of others. It made me feel better about myself.

(He gasps and breathes into the mask several times.)

Love is a hard thing to learn when you've only known heartache. I ain't makin' excuses. There was a dark pit in me that could never be filled. I was mean like my old man. That's how I grew up. That's what I was taught. Now, this fella come to school with a class project. He must've spent days workin' on it. You could see the attention to detail. I saw him walkin' to school with it, so I thought I'd have some fun. Couple of the other fellas were right there when I tripped him to the ground. His project broke and scattered everywhere. He started cryin' and I laughed in his face.

(He gasps and breathes into the mask several times.)

I never saw that fella again. My old man threw me out of the house 'cause I was skippin' work and school. Said I could make my own way. I was thirteen years old. I cried. Only time ever.

(He gasps and breathes into the mask several times.)

I went to them rail tracks and looked in both directions. I had only two choices. Go east or west. I caught that mighty old train callin' to me and hoboed my way west. I found work on them tracks, too. Built myself a future. I was a railroad man all my life. Every now and then when I see our paperboy droppin' my newspaper on my steps, I'm reminded of that fella I tormented long ago. I wonder whatever became of him. I wonder if he ever thinks of me. Age has softened my meanness. What I did to that fella wasn't right. When I think about it, I feel like a thirteen-year-old all over again. I wish I could tell that fella "I'm sorry. Real sorry." We reap what we sow, you know?

(He gasps and breathes into the mask several times.)

Charlie's Angel

(YOUNG WOMAN stands, holding an unopened envelope in her hand.)

YOUNG WOMAN. My best friend Amy spread a rumor about me that was untrue. She did it as a joke and then it got out of hand. She told everyone I was a wild girl and loved to party with boys. Pretty soon I was known as "T Girl." The "T" stood for "Tramp."

(She looks at the envelope.)

"T Girl" became my permanent nickname at school. I'd have to live with that name until I graduated from school. When I think back, I wanted to be like Farrah Fawcett. She was in the original *Charlie's Angels*. She was beautiful and had this amazing hairstyle to die for. After my nickname stuck, I tried to disappear into the school walls and into my books so no one would see me and call me that name. It didn't work. I was so hurt and embarrassed that I stopped talking to people and I stayed by myself. My grades suffered and my mom couldn't crack me open. I even thought about taking pills once.

(She looks at the envelope again.)

I'm a grandmother now. My daughter gave birth to a beautiful little girl named Emily. She's the apple of my eye.

(She tears open the envelope.)

My old school is holding a thirty-five-year reunion. I just got the invitation. Will I go? No. I can never go back there. Too much water under the bridge. I couldn't stand people calling me "T Girl" again. That time of growing up was important to me. And what Amy did made an imprint on my soul forever. I can never forgive her.

(She tears the envelope in half.)

Every now and then I have this reoccurring dream where I play Jill Monroe, the Farrah Fawcett character in the original *Charlie's Angels*. I find myself at school with my bellbottom pants and cool top and gorgeous Jill Monroe hairstyle and karate chop and kick every person that ever called me "T Girl." As I turn to leave, I flip my hair back like Farrah did and walk away looking gorgeous. It's only a dream, but it brings a smile to me.

(She poses like the three women from the Charlie's Angels *iconic image.)*

Monster

(MONSTER, a teen boy, stands, carrying a briefcase.)

MONSTER. I dreamed of being rich, important and popular. I got the first two. Everything I learned, I learned in school, but not from the classroom. I learned that there are monsters roaming the hallways, cafeterias and play-grounds, looking to eat you up like Godzilla did to Japan. In their wake of destruction, monsters can make other monsters. I'm a monster. I wasn't one, but I am now. I'm rich and important, but not popular. I go for what I want and I don't care who gets in my way or who gets hurt. In business, you got to be a monster. I'm thankful now for the monster that made me a monster. I used to be inno-cent, trusting and friendly, but to monsters that is a sign of weakness. Monsters will eat you alive. That's what happened to me. I was eaten alive, but I survived and learned from it. It made me stronger. I have no weakness.

I make other monsters now. People fear me and that's the way I like it.

(He opens his briefcase.)

I was a momma's boy. Always dressed nice with my hair combed to one side. My mom always prepared me a sack lunch. I was good in school, but I didn't become a monster right away. You see, it takes time to transform into one. The longer the change the stronger you'll be. Many years later I found the monster that turned me into a monster. He was grown up and was working as an employee for a small transportation company. Well, I bought and sold that company off in pieces making me a nice little bundle. I can't tell you what joy that brought me. He was married with three kids and had a mortgage. I saw him cry and the monster in me celebrated.

(He holds up a plastic Godzilla toy.)

Monsters aren't extinct. We're still roaming the earth.

END OF PLAY

Glorious Gail

By Max Bush

CHARACTERS

SETTING AND TIME: The beach on Lake Michigan, the rooms of three high-school students. June of this year.

Scene 1

(MUSIC. BECKY, KATHY and MIKE sit in the dark, frozen, looking into their laptop webcams or camcorders during the first scene.

LIGHTS isolate the beach in the morning, in mid-June. On the ground, facing away from us, unconscious, is GAIL. She wears pants, sandals and a blouse, but the blouse is pulled down about two inches in the back. Also, she wears a clown-like wig.

For a few moments she is alone onstage with the SOUND of waves and gulls.

NICK, tall and athletic, runs on.)

NICK. Gail? Gail! We've been looking all over for you. *(GAIL moans. MUSIC out.)* What are you doing out here? *(She begins to stir, groans.)* Where were you all night? And what's with the hair? *(He's moving around behind her.)* Your mother called me this morning, yelling at me because— *(He stops abruptly when he sees her face. He begins to laugh, but quickly stops. He takes her in, bends down, shakes her.)* Gail…Gail, are you all right? *(He turns her on her back.)* What the hell is this? *(A bouquet of wilted and torn flowers is tucked inside her belt at the navel. He takes flowers out, tosses them away.)* Gail! *(He looks her up and down.)* Gail! Are you hurt?

GAIL. Nick?

NICK. What happened to you? Where have you been?

GAIL. What am I…

(GAIL sits up, clutches her side. She faces out. We now see what NICK reacted to. GAIL's face is grotesquely made up—a cross between an overly made-up prostitute and a clown. The foundation makeup is very light and smeared unevenly. The rest of the makeup is thick and hurriedly smeared. Her blouse is pulled down—not revealing breasts—but enough so the word "SLUT" could be written across her upper chest in large, red letters. The work "PIG" is written on her forehead. The word "SINS" is written on her right arm near the wrist, and the word "BITCH" is written on her left forearm.)

NICK. Are you hurt somewhere?

GAIL. My ribs…my neck…my face… What happened?

NICK. I don't know, I just found you here. Where were you all night?

GAIL *(looks around, confused)*. The beach? I'm on the beach?

NICK. Yeah, the beach. It's Wednesday morning. You've been gone all night. What the hell happened, Gail?

GAIL. But how— *(She starts to move, clutches her side; she's beginning to panic.)* Ah! How did I get here?

NICK. I'm going to call an ambulance, all right? You don't look good.

GAIL. Who brought me here?

NICK *(takes out his phone)*. You don't know how you got here?

GAIL. Nick, what happened?

NICK. Maybe you should just not move, you know, relax, babe.

GAIL. It's Wednesday?

NICK. Yeah, about 9:30 in the morning.

GAIL *(looks at her arm, reads it)*. What... "SINS"... Does this say "SINS"? *(She looks at her other arm.)* "BITCH." Who wrote this on my arm? *(Looking down at herself, sees something written on her chest.)* What?... What does this say?

NICK. Relax, babe, I don't think you should move. You're hurtin.' And—

GAIL. What does it say?!

NICK. Just relax. Let me call an ambulance. *(He dials his phone.)*

GAIL *(frantic)*. What happened to me? Who did this? *(She sees the hair on her head is not her own; she pulls off the wig, looks at it.)* Who did this to me?!

(LIGHTS crossfade to a half-light on NICK and GAIL as he helps her up and off.)

Scene 2

(Three separate areas are lit, revealing three separate scenes. KATHY, BECKY and MIKE are in the separate areas, each setting up a laptop webcam or camcorder. They will each stand, face their individual cameras and talk to them.

KATHY finishes setting up first and begins. The others will follow.)

KATHY. Hello again, friends. I cannot believe what I have for you today. It's either hilarious or terrifying, I'm not sure. Last night I drove out to The Point with my boyfriend—Hulk—and as we drove up, we saw something on the ground. We found—I'm not making this up—photographs—the pics on the left.

MIKE. Oh, man, you got to see this. I scored these pictures last night at The Café. When the waitress at the coffee shop showed us to our table, there on my chair were these pictures. Check it out. *(Holds up an 8 x 10.)*

BECKY. And as we came out of the movies, I saw these photographs tucked in my windshield. *(Holding up an 8 x 10.)*

KATHY. My boyfriend found the pictures seriously addictive and more interesting than a saucy and amorous me. But who could blame him?

MIKE. Do you know what you're looking at?

KATHY. This is going to be famous.

BECKY. Going to be priceless.

MIKE. On the top it says:

BECKY. "Beach Party."

KATHY. "Beach Party"!

KATHY. On the bottom it says:

BECKY. "Who is this?"

MIKE. At first I couldn't tell.

KATHY. "Who is this?"

MIKE. She was wearing a wig.

KATHY. At first I questioned her hair skills but—

BECKY. I looked closer and saw it was—

KATHY. [Gasp.]

BECKY. Gail Van Ess.

MIKE & KATHY. Gail Van Ess!

MIKE. And she was looking *fine*.

BECKY. *Was* this a party?

MIKE. A beach party?

BECKY. It looks like Crystal Beach.

KATHY. Had she had A-Special-Kind-Of-Party?

MIKE. A party that I hadn't been invited to.

KATHY. Were any of you there?

BECKY. What party game was this?

MIKE. How could I not be invited to this party!

KATHY. What I hope is

BECKY. Maybe she

MIKE. She passed out.

KATHY. Her friends

MIKE. Her friends made her up.

BECKY. Her friends wanted everyone to know "who this is."

KATHY. But then, these words—

MIKE. Would her friends—

KATHY. These aren't party words—

MIKE. I don't know if friends would write—

KATHY. It's a little difficult, but I think you can see all four:

BECKY *(indicating on her forehead)*. "Pig"

MIKE *(indicating on her chest)*. "Slut."

BECKY *(indicating on her arm)*. "Sins."

KATHY *(indicating on her arm)*. "Bitch."

BECKY. To be fair, I've never known her to be a slut.

MIKE. Or I would have been knocking on her door.

KATHY. With who?

MIKE. All right, I did knock on that door, but she never—

BECKY. Who knows what happens at night,

MIKE. All right,

BECKY. What secrets she has.

MIKE. I'd give her my *truck* if she would go out with me.

BECKY. Anyone with personal experience?

MIKE. And "Sins"?

KATHY. What sins?

BECKY. Gail has special sins?

MIKE. I want a photo of those sins!

BECKY. What sins, how sins?

MIKE. "Sins," I don't know, and

BECKY. "Pig"?

KATHY. Pig, in what—am I dense?

BECKY. Pig, in what way?

KATHY. But Beeyotch.

MIKE. Rich Bitch.

BECKY. That fits.

MIKE. Straight up. Glorious Gail. Rich Bitch. But would her friends—

KATHY. Would her party friends—

MIKE. Maybe it wasn't a party—

BECKY. —would be so angry

KATHY. Violent.

MIKE. Has anybody seen her?

BECKY. PIG, SLUT, .

MIKE. Is she all right?

BECKY. SINS, BITCH.

MIKE. Somebody call her, let me know.

KATHY. Is this about the beach?

MIKE. About her family developing the beach?

KATHY. There's a sin.

BECKY. About destroying Crystal Beach?

MIKE. Attack the beach, attack her?

KATHY. Please let me know.

BECKY. Questions, questions, who has an answer to—

MIKE. Find me, talk to me, tell me.

BECKY. Check back to see what—

MIKE. Gotta be clear, man, because you—

KATHY. Lots of love, Kathy. *(Lights fade out on KATHY.)*

MIKE. Have something to say.

BECKY. Respectfully submitted, Rebecca Barnes. *(LIGHTS fade out on BECKY.)*

MIKE. All right. I'm out. Peace. *(LIGHTS out on MIKE.)*

(Beat. Another beat. LIGHTS suddenly come up on the three BLOGGERS again.)

BECKY. Faithful friends, you will be rewarded.

KATHY. I know it's been two weeks, dear friends, but something just came in the mail, today,

MIKE. Back on the front page,

KATHY. To my very house!

BECKY. Something old but new, something—

MIKE. I got this envelope in the mail and—

KATHY. In the mail this time—

BECKY. I had to show you because—

KATHY. What are these photographs—I am afraid—about?

MIKE. When I opened the envelope,

KATHY. Two new pictures of—

MIKE. You can't see her face, but

BECKY. Two different photographs.

KATHY. [Gasp!] Gail Van Ess,

MIKE. Gail Van Ess,

KATHY. Again!

BECKY. The same top,

MIKE. Same clothes as in the other.

BECKY. Can you see?

MIKE. Close up on her stomach,

KATHY. Over her, like—

BECKY. Written in black, on her belly—

MIKE. In black it says: "Dead."

BECKY. "Dead."

KATHY. They wrote "Dead."

BECKY. Meaning her womb is dead?

KATHY. An abortion?

MIKE. Like an abortion?

BECKY. "Dead" meaning "Lifeless"?

MIKE. Did Gail Van Ess have an abortion?

KATHY. Does anyone—somebody has to—know?

MIKE. But who would be the would-be dad?

KATHY. John?

MIKE. Then who would have a reason to—

KATHY. Nick?

MIKE. Then gimme a sign so I can—

KATHY. You?

BECKY. Is that why Nick punched John in the—

MIKE. Yeah.

KATHY. Why Nick pummeled John inside the cafe

MIKE. Yeah!

BECKY. I want some pics of John's bloody face.

(Short silence.)

KATHY. An abortion…Gail…last month she was out of algebra class for a week…

(Short silence.)

MIKE. And what about the other

BECKY. The other photograph

KATHY. On her—what is that?—back?

BECKY. Her blouse is pulled up.

MIKE. Hiked up, so we can see

BECKY. On her back they wrote in red

KATHY. Written in evil red:

MIKE. "Rapist"

BECKY. "Rapist," but the S is a dollar sign.

KATHY. "Rapist," and they made the S into a—this says something—dollar sign.

MIKE. That's got to be about the beach

KATHY. About the dunes.

MIKE. About the family

BECKY. About developing the beach.

MIKE. About raping the dunes. *(Short silence.)* Who sent me these?

KATHY. John?

MIKE. Do you have any more?

KATHY. John Anderson?

MIKE. You got to have more.

KATHY. Did you send—

MIKE. And why did—

BECKY. Write me something,

MIKE. Write me, talk to me, tell me

KATHY. What exactly

MIKE. Rapist-Pig-Sins-Dead—

KATHY. Are you trying to say?

(Short silence.)

BECKY. Why isn't Gail talking?

KATHY. Why don't we know—

MIKE. Who does she think—

BECKY. What does she—
MIKE. No one arrested.
BECKY. She's been seen, but hasn't said
MIKE. So I got to ask
BECKY. Has anyone thought—
MIKE. Did this happen?
BECKY. Did Gail send me these photos?
MIKE. Did anyone actually do this?

(Beat.)

KATHY. Gail-Gail—
BECKY. Gail—
MIKE. Gail-Gail—
KATHY. Glorious Gail! Why are
BECKY. You
MIKE. A PIG!?

(Short silence.)

KATHY. As darkness descends on Crystal Beach
BECKY. What do you think?
KATHY. I have to think of Gail. And you, who sent these
pictures—I probably know you! And I have to think of
words that we haven't seen written on anybody—yet.
Words like "revenge."
BECKY. Post your comments.
KATHY. And "hate." Will we see these?
MIKE. Step out of the shadows, man.
KATHY. What is going on inside you?
MIKE. Step up, tell me straight,
BECKY. I'll keep digging.
MIKE. If you're even out there.
KATHY. Lots of love,

MIKE. 'Cause, who knows Gail Van Ess?
BECKY. I'll have an update soon.
MIKE. And what she would do.
BECKY. Respectfully submitted,
MIKE. All right. I'm out.
BECKY. Rebecca Barnes.
MIKE. Peace.

(DIM OUT.)

END OF PLAY

Happy Birthday, Heather Higby (I Am Plotting Your Doom)

By Stephen Gregg

CHARACTERS

MERCY NIGHTINGALE .... a student
CHARLENE.. a student
HEATHER HIGBY... a student
MONSTER HEATHER ....a monster (non-speaking)
TEACHERS (two)
A MECHANICAL VOICE .... (offstage)
SPIES (at least two)
RUMORS, RUMOR HANDLER
PASSERBY STUDENT, SECOND PASSERBY

(LIGHTS up on a cupcake with a candle in it, sitting on a pedestal.)

MERCY *(enters; speaks directly to audience)*. All right, everyone, listen up. My name is Mercy Nightingale. I have brought you here under false pretenses. This is not actually a play. This is more like a trap. Every single person here is going to help me destroy my arch-nemesis, Heather Higby.
SPY ONE *(enters)*. Eight minutes!
MERCY. Thank you.

(MERCY has a stopwatch, which she sets. SPY ONE exits.)

MERCY *(cont'd)*. Heather is on her way here even as I speak, so we'll need to move fast. Here is a quick lesson on what we're doing and who we're doing it to. This is Heather Higby.

(MONSTER HEATHER enters. While MERCY introduces her, CHARLENE enters, casually replaces the candle in the cupcake. She exits without MERCY having noticed.)

MERCY *(cont'd)*. This is not actually Heather. This is a more appealing stand-in. Note the crazed expression in the eyes. *(MONSTER HEATHER obliges with a crazed expression.)* Note also Heather's claws, useful for stabbing people in the back. *(MONSTER HEATHER reveals claws.)* And of course, the fangs, designed to make sure something unpleasant happens every time she opens her mouth. *(MONSTER HEATHER reveals her horrible fangs.)* Say hello, Heather. *(MONSTER HEATHER snarls loud and long.)* This is a birthday cake. Today, [this day's date] isn't Heather's birthday in the traditional sense. Your birthday isn't only the day you're born. Your birthday is also the day that people start to see you for who you really are.

CHARLENE *(enters)*. Excuse me.

MERCY. Yes?

CHARLENE. I hate to be—you jumped the gun. You're on next. After us.

MERCY. No.

CHARLENE. Yeah, you are. Check the program. *(She has a program with her, or borrows one from the audience.)*

My play—it's actually more like performance art—is called *Sparks*. It's scheduled right before yours.

MERCY. Yes, Charlene, and look at the bottom, where it says "Order of plays subject to change."

CHARLENE. Well, my mom has to visit my aunt, who's sick, so I have to get home to watch my little sister.

MERCY. We already started.

CHARLENE. I know.

MERCY. Plus, my timing is crucial. I have a "guest" arriving in six minutes and thirteen seconds.

CHARLENE. Well we can do our plays side by side. You know, sort of alternate scenes.

MERCY. That's not gonna work.

CHARLENE. I already got Mrs. Persimmon's [or an actual teacher's] permission.

MERCY. She's not here.

CHARLENE. She will be if I call her and tell her what you're doing.

MERCY. What's your art thing about?

CHARLENE. Gossip and rumors.

MERCY. All right, that's not an excellent companion piece, theme-wise.

CHARLENE. Actually it sort of is.

MERCY. No.

CHARLENE. I'm taking the pro-position.

MERCY. Pro?

CHARLENE. Uh-huh. I'm all for spreading rumors. I think we should gossip more.

MERCY. You're right, this could work. Spies! *(The SPIES enter.)* These are my spies. Spy One.

SPY ONE *(says his/her first name)*. Hi.

MERCY. And Spy Two.

SPY TWO. Hey there. *(Says his/her first name.)* A spy.

MERCY. I need a few extra minutes. Find a way to slow down Heather.

SPY TWO. Done.

(The SPIES exit.)

MERCY. So, what? We alternate scenes?

CHARLENE. Uh-huh. Are you done with your intro?

MERCY. No.

CHARLENE. No sweat. I'll wait offstage. Just tell me my cue.

MERCY. Your cue is: I blow out this candle.

CHARLENE. Got it.

(CHARLENE exits. MERCY lights the cupcake candle.)

MERCY. Right now, the main thing I need you to notice about Heather is the smile. She smiles constantly. She is filled with annoying happiness, and it's our job to fix that. Heather, I congratulate you on your optimistic, sunny point of view. It is that point of view that I am going to use to crush you. So happy birthday, Heather Higby. I am plotting your doom. *(She blows out the candle.)* That's <u>doom</u>. *(Spells it:)* D-O-O-O-M. **DOOOOM.**

(The candle relights. She blows it out again. It relights. She blows it out. It relights. CHARLENE enters.)

CHARLENE. So. Is it our turn, yet?

MERCY. Not quite, obviously.

CHARLENE. Well, like you said, we're running out of time.

MERCY *(makes one more attempt to blow out the candle)*. Just go. *(She turns the candle over and puts it out in the

cupcake. *To someone offstage.)* WHERE DID THIS
CANDLE COME FROM? *(To CHARLENE.)* What's my
cue to come back?
CHARLENE. You'll hear a buzzer.

*(MERCY exits. MONSTER HEATHER stays onstage for
most of the play.)*

CHARLENE *(cont'd, to the audience).* My performance
piece, *Sparks*, is about rumors and gossip. Teachers tell
students not to spread rumors but that's ridiculous. The
same teachers who tell us not to gossip, gossip about each
other all the time. I planted a spy camera in the teacher's
lounge. This is video from that camera. I have removed
offensive material and obscured the identities of all
concerned.

*(Two TEACHERS enter. Something obscures their faces,
mimicking the effect that television uses to smear out
faces. [See Notes.])*

TEACHER ONE. Hello Mr. **GONG**!
TEACHER TWO. Hi Mrs. **BEEEEEP.**
TEACHER ONE. Have you heard about Ms.—

*(The characters freeze for a moment while the
MECHANICAL VOICE fills in.)*

MECHANICAL VOICE. —or Mr.—
TEACHER ONE. **SLIDE WHISTLE**?
TEACHER TWO. No, what about her—
MECHANICAL VOICE. —or him.
TEACHER ONE. **SLIDE WHISTLE** is dating **SCREAM**.
TEACHER TWO. **SCREAM?** Are you sure?

TEACHER ONE. Positive. I saw them at the movies together.

TEACHER TWO. *No.*

TEACHER ONE. Yes! They were holding hands.

TEACHER TWO. Holy **CUCKOO!** Does **OPERA NOTE** know?

TEACHER ONE. **OPERA NOTE** *introduced* them.

TEACHER TWO. Wow. I thought he—

MECHANICAL VOICE. Or she—

TEACHER TWO. Was interested in **SCREAM** him—

MECHANICAL VOICE. Or her—

TEACHER TWO. Self.

TEACHER ONE. I thought so too.

TEACHER TWO. **BIRD CHIRP.** Honest to **CUCKOO HICCUP BUZZER.**

(MERCY enters as the TEACHERS exit. CHARLENE stays onstage, discreetly to the side.)

MERCY *(to audience)*. My Heather revenge consists of three parts. Part one is devastating. Part two is extra devastating. And part three is my patented ultimate revenge of destroying doom. For the last week, my spies have been collecting information. They've been talking to people who know Heather now, and who knew her in the past: enemies and frenemies and people with secret grudges. My spies are making lists of everything Heather doesn't want known about her, every unkind thing she's done or said, every embarrassing secret. And when Heather arrives here, they're going to tell us all of these things. The only thing better than revenge is public revenge, humiliation in front of an audience. *But*, before public humiliation comes private fear. Part one: Paranoia.

Heather starts to worry that people are talking about her *because they are*. It's easy to do. Bring it on!

(The RUMOR, an ugly dark shape enters. Perhaps it has a beak. It's held in check by a RUMOR HANDLER, who has it on a long leash, or perhaps in chains.)

CHARLENE. Is that what I think it is?
MERCY. Why are you still onstage?
CHARLENE. What is that?
MERCY. It's a rumor.
CHARLENE. That's what I thought.

(The RUMOR hisses at MONSTER HEATHER, who recoils.)

CHARLENE *(cont'd)*. That's an awfully mean rumor.
MERCY. Thank you.
CHARLENE. You don't really want to release that thing.
MERCY. Yes I do.
CHARLENE. What good will that do?
MERCY. It'll hurt Heather.
CHARLENE. I said what *good* will it do?
MERCY. And I told you, it'll hurt Heather. *(She shows off the RUMOR, the way a car salesperson would.)* Look how solidly built it is. This is one rumor guaranteed to travel and travel and just keep traveling.
CHARLENE. Mercy, please don't put that thing out into the world.
MERCY. Why shouldn't I? Huh? *(Beat.)* I asked you a question.
CHARLENE. Heather's a friend of mine.
MERCY. I know that. Of course I know that. *(Beat.)* I thought you were all *for* rumors.

CHARLENE. This one's too ugly.

MERCY. No such thing as too ugly. *(To the RUMOR HANDLER.)* Go ahead.

(The RUMOR HANDLER lets the RUMOR go. It moves, slowly at first, then faster.)

CHARLENE. Stop!

(No reaction. The RUMOR just keeps going.)

MERCY. You can't stop it. Watch what happens when it finds someone it likes.

(A PASSERBY STUDENT enters, perhaps reading a book or texting. The STUDENT doesn't see the RUMOR. The RUMOR approaches, startling the STUDENT at first. Then the STUDENT examines it, and as s/he does so, it whispers in their ear, and—a slightly different, even SCARIER VERSION of the RUMOR enters.)

CHARLENE. Oh no.

MERCY. Yup. It multiplies.

CHARLENE. That one's a little different.

MERCY. It changes as it spreads.

(More RUMORS enter, each more horrible than the last.)

CHARLENE. They're getting uglier.

MERCY. Uglier and meaner. That's by design.

(One of the RUMORS swipes at MONSTER HEATHER, who reacts with real pain. Another one of the RUMORS starts to wobble, stops moving.)

PASSERBY STUDENT. That one's almost dead.

MERCY. It happens sometimes. But you can usually find someone to feed it.

(A SECOND PASSERBY enters, sees the RUMOR. The SECOND PASSERBY starts to retch. Again and again until s/he coughs up something into his/her hand. It's a worm. S/he dangles it in front of the DYING RUMOR.)

CHARLENE. Ew. What is that?

MERCY. It's a Don't Tell Anyworm.

(The SECOND PASSERBY lowers the worm toward the snapping beak of the DYING RUMOR. As s/he does, we hear whispers: "Don't tell anyone! Don't tell anyone. Don't. Tell. Anyone." The DYING RUMOR swallows the worm, is suddenly full of vitality.)

CHARLENE. Why are you doing this?

MERCY *(to the RUMORS)*. Follow me! *(The RUMORS ignore her.)* I said follow me!

(Still nothing. It takes her a bit, but MERCY manages to retch up a Don't Tell Anyworm. She dangles it as bait. We hear it whispering: "Don't tell anyone! Don't tell anyone..." as the rabid RUMORS follow her offstage. CHARLENE and the PASSERBY STUDENT watch them, simultaneously mesmerized and repelled. Finally CHARLENE regains her composure enough to address the audience.)

CHARLENE. You can't stop people from gossiping. It's like trying to stop them from breathing. But sometimes if you can't stop something, you can change it. Once in a while, slow down, look around, and spread a rumor about someone that they'd actually want people to hear. *(Beat.)* Mercy Nightingale is a bully, but she has a little brother, Martin, who has trouble in school, and every night she sits with him, and helps him with his homework, and reminds him that he's smart.

(We hear a MUSICAL NOTE, as a spark appears, hovers and flits, and then disappears.)

PASSERBY STUDENT. Do that again.

CHARLENE. Mercy is good to her little brother. *(Again, a MUSICAL NOTE, and a spark.)* Good rumors are like sparks. They provide light, and heat if there are enough of them. They let us see better and help to keep us warm.

MERCY *(storms onto the stage).* I'm not a bully! I'm an avenging angel! How do you know about my brother?

CHARLENE. I have my own spies. *(A stray RUMOR wanders by. It has a leash. CHARLENE picks up the leash.)* Hey. You. Slow down. *(The RUMOR pulls her relentlessly.)* Stop. *(As she's dragged offstage:)* I said stop!

MERCY. Part two of my plan. Meanaphormosis! Meanaphormosis is the art of saying something nice while making it cruel. When you speak to Heather, no matter what you say, you can say it with cruelty built right in. If used properly this technique is devastating and untraceable. I need three volunteers. You have to be able to read. Raise your hands! NOW. You. You. And you. *(She hands each of the VOLUNTEERS sealed pieces of paper.)* Open your papers when I say so. Meanamorphosis is a skill. Like any skill, it takes practice. When you open your paper, you are to read it and say it as meanly as possible. *(To the first VOLUNTEER.)* Are you ready? Go.

VOLUNTEER ONE *(opens the paper. It says:)*. Hello.

MERCY. Meaner.

VOLUNTEER ONE. Hello.

MERCY. Meaner! *(To the second VOLUNTEER.)* Your turn. All the cruelty you can muster. Are you ready?

VOLUNTEER TWO *(opens their paper. It says:)*. Which way is the library?

(MERCY is impressed or not. If not, she makes them practice once or twice.)

MERCY *(to the third VOLUNTEER)*. And finally you. Say this sentence in a way that will cause Heather's teeth to fall out.

VOLUNTEER THREE *(opens their envelope and reads. It says:)*. Thank you for donating me that kidney.

MERCY. *Meaner!*

VOLUNTEER THREE. Thank you for donating me that kidney.

MERCY Amateur! Watch and learn. *(She turns to MONSTER HEATHER.)* Hello! *(MONSTER HEATHER flinches.)* Which way is the library? *(MONSTER HEATHER flinches even more.)* Thank you for donating me that kidney. *(MONSTER HEATHER yelps in pain.)* That's how you do it!

(SPY TWO enters, followed by CHARLENE.)

SPY TWO. She's on her way! Heather's doom in t-minus eighty-one seconds!

MERCY. Excellent!

(SPY TWO exits.)

CHARLENE. It's my turn.

MERCY. We're canceling your turn. In seventy-four seconds, we're destroying Heather Higby. And there's nothing you can do about it.

CHARLENE. Can I ask you something?

MERCY. Quickly.

CHARLENE. What exactly did Heather do to you?

MERCY *(loses a bit of her edge, perhaps becomes a little less sure of herself)*. It's not…

CHARLENE. What?

MERCY. It's not any one thing. It's more like a…you know she has all these friends and…they're always together. And they don't say hi to you, and…you know. You can just tell that they…

CHARLENE. That they what?

MERCY. You can tell that part of what's fun for them about being friends together is that they're not friends with you.

CHARLENE. That sounds awful.

MERCY. You're one of them.

CHARLENE. Oh.

MERCY. Yeah.

CHARLENE. Huh.

MERCY. Yeah. Not even, like, a hello in the hall.

CHARLENE. You don't say hello, either.

MERCY. You're with a whole group.

CHARLENE *(ponders this for a moment, gets it)*. I'm sorry.

MERCY. It's Heather who's about to be sorry. In thirty-one seconds.

CHARLENE. I wonder if it would help if you knew some things about Heather.

MERCY. It wouldn't.

CHARLENE. It might.

MERCY. Too late. Heather is going to be here in fourteen seconds.

CHARLENE. Still, I wish you'd let me tell you some things.

MERCY. You've run out of time. ...Six. Five. Four. Three. Two. One. *(A long moment.)* HELLO?!

CHARLENE. I intercepted your spies. Your spies are double agents. They've been secretly working for me. Spies!

(The SPIES enter.)

MERCY. What do you mean, they've been working for you?

CHARLENE. They've been finding out things about Heather, just like you wanted. Only these are good things. Things that Heather would want known.

SPY TWO. Heather Higby won second place in the shotput in only the second meet she ever entered. *(MUSICAL NOTE, spark.)*

SPY ONE. When she was ten, Heather Higby rescued a dog, an older dog, and gave it a good home. *(MUSICAL NOTE, spark.)*

SPY TWO. Heather volunteers at a book fair once a month. *(MUSICAL NOTE, spark.)*

SPY ONE. And here's something else good about Heather Higby. Heather once defended you in conversation.

MERCY. Defended how?

SPY ONE. Someone told her that you'd said mean things about her.

MERCY. Well, that might have almost been true.

SPY TWO. Heather said that that probably wasn't your best moment. Then she told us about your brother.

(Extra long MUSICAL NOTE, extra long-lasting spark.)

MERCY. How did she know about my brother?

SPY ONE. Your brother gossiped about you.

SPY TWO. People have been talking about you behind your back, but in a good way.

(MONSTER HEATHER exits.)

SPY TWO *(cont'd)*. Heather's entered the building.

CHARLENE. But my spies didn't stop with Heather. They burrowed through the school, quietly, asking questions, digging for information about other people as well.

SPY ONE. Here's a rumor that you could spread. This rumor is about someone in the audience right now: *(S/he tells the good thing about the audience member.)*

SPY TWO. Here's another one. *[Audience member]*, here right now: *(S/he tells the good rumor.)* Bet you didn't know that, but now you can tell people.

CHARLENE. Your birthday is the day that people start to see you for what you really are.

SPY ONE. One more. Here's something you might know about *[audience member]*, sitting over there: *(S/he tells the rumor.)*

(HEATHER enters, a little tentatively, since she's walking into the middle of a performance.)

CHARLENE. Hey, Heather.

HEATHER. Hey. Is this—they said it was OK to just come onstage.

MERCY. Yeah, it's OK.

CHARLENE. We were just talking about you.

HEATHER. Oh yeah. About what?

(There's a long moment. The LIGHTS start to fade.)

CHARLENE. It was actually Mercy who was doing most of the talking.
HEATHER. What were you saying?
MERCY. I was saying... *(The LIGHTS keep fading.)* Uh...well, actually, what we were saying was...

(The LIGHTS are almost gone. MERCY opens her mouth. A spark flies out. Then another. We hear MUSICAL NOTES as—sparks fill the air.)

END OF PLAY

NOTES

First: <u>To do this play, you need the permission and cooperation of your theatre teacher</u>.

To the Spies: You are the key to this play. It's up to you to find out, any way you can, things about your audience members that would make us like them. You'll have to be creative and clever.

The thing you're looking for can be a little-known accomplishment, or a talent, or something that the person did: a kindness ongoing or from the past.

But the job doesn't end there.

The hardest part of your job isn't gathering the rumors. It's deciding—*in conjunction with your teacher*—whether it's a good idea to say them out loud in a performance. There are plenty of people—I count myself among them—who would hate being named for any reason in front of an audience.

And, sad to say, there are plenty of wonderful things about students in your audience that might not get the hoped-for reaction from the rest of the audience. The worst possible result of performing *Heather Higby* would be to call unwanted attention to a vulnerable student.

Consider the climate of the school you'll be performing at. Is it warm, or is it snarky?

Err on the side of not naming individuals.

A perfectly good, just as effective, way to produce the play is to not name audience members at all but to make all the rumors, and all the sparks, be about Heather.

At the very least, you and the rest of the cast will have discovered wonderful things about members of your audience, and that's what's important. This play won't change the climate of your school, but you can.

Of course, if you're touring this play or other considerations make it impossible to gather good rumors, just make up a rumor or two more about Heather.

For Theatre Teachers: There's a section of my website, Stephengreggplays.com, called *Spark*s. When you click on it, you get an explanation of what it is and a listing of all the good things that have been learned about people during the preproduction of *Heather Higby*.

If you'd like, get your students' permission and then send me your name and the name, city and state of your school along with the names of the people you honored and the good thing that you said about them. I'll post the names on the site, along with the rumors.

Effects: Monster Heather is probably played by a guy in a bad wig. She probably has monstrous features other than those mentioned.

If you can do so safely, and if your school will allow it, a laser pointer is a good way to make sparks. But you can also use a spotlight. Or a mirror ball.

If it's too hard to manage, you can change sparks into musical notes and change the dialogue to match. Charlene's play is called *Notes*. "Good rumors are like musical notes. They brighten the world and make it seem less scary."

When thinking about sound effects for the teachers, consider having the cast members make them vocally. If well done, it's quite funny.

A perfectly good way to obscure teacher's faces would be a fan, probably made from wire and covered in cellophane or wax paper.

Put a good chunk of your resources—imaginative or otherwise—into costuming the Rumors. Monster Heather is monstrous in a comic way but the rumors should be scary, if possible.

Ideally, you'll get real volunteers from the audience, but you'd better have a back-up plan involving the actors who aren't onstage.

If you can wrangle them and you're performing it at your school, it might be fun to use real teachers.

Of course, whenever you work with real audience members, flexibility is key. It couldn't hurt to brush up on your improv skills.

Her

By Geraldine Ann Snyder

CHARACTERS

MICHAEL T. .... a high-school student
AMY .... a high-school student
JO-LETTE .... a high-school student
DEENA .... a high-school student
DARIUS .... a high-school student

SETTING AND TIME: A school ground. The present.

(LIGHTS up. Enter MICHAEL T. and AMY.)

MICHAEL T. Come on, Amy. Deena can't be that mad at me.
AMY. Don't count on it, Michael T. She pretty much *is*!

(Enter JO-LETTE.)

AMY *(cont'd)*. She saw you talking to HER at lunch.
MICHAEL T. I just asked the pig to get out of my way. That's *all*.
AMY. That's not the way Deena saw it.
JO-LETTE. That's not the way I saw it either, Michael T.
MICHAEL T. You have got to be kidding, Jo-Lette!
AMY. What else were you talking about?
JO-LETTE. Deena wants to know.

167

MICHAEL T. Everybody knows she hooks up with *everybody*. So what?

AMY. So *what*!

JO-LETTE. Deena thinks *you* hooked up with her, too.

MICHAEL T. So what if I did? I don't owe Deena anything.

AMY. She thinks you do. And she's about to pound into HER once and for all. Word gets around and Deena's had about enough!

MICHAEL T. Deena's gonna do what she wants to do. Let her. It will be fun to watch.

JO-LETTE. Look!… Way over there, it's HER!

MICHAEL T. It's everybody's "Ho"!

JO-LETTE. She's lucky Deena's not here. She might not have that dumb smile on her face.

AMY. Were you there when Marvin spit on her in homeroom?

(ALL laugh.)

JO-LETTE. She had crap hanging down the back of her hair all day! It was great!

MICHAEL T. Great? Unless you sat behind her in class!

ALL. Ooo-ooo-ooo!

AMY. Darius sits behind her in history. He even managed to put three toothpicks in her hair!

JO-LETTE. That's when everybody started calling her "the porcupine"!

(ALL laugh.)

MICHAEL T. She's so stupid. She didn't have a clue. It's been fun all day!

AMY. How long is it going to take Darius to get here? I need a ride.

JO-LETTE. I thought I was gonna get a ride, too. I could have gotten on the bus and been home by now.

MICHAEL T. He has last period with Deena. And you know Deena!

AMY. She probably *had* to go back to her locker "Just to get…

ALL. …one or two things!"

JO-LETTE. In that case, this could take forever.

AMY. Not again! She's got to start writing herself *notes* or something!

JO-LETTE. This is ridiculous! Every day!

MICHAEL T. Hey, look over there! The Ho's coming this way.

AMY. Oh my god! I can even see the toothpicks from here.

JO-LETTE. So can I!

AMY. The crap is still in the porcupine's hair!

(ALL laugh. Enter DARIUS and DEENA.)

AMY *(cont'd)*. Can you believe it?

DEENA. What's so funny, everybody?

JO-LETTE *(pointing)*. Look, Deena. It's HER!

DARIUS. No, don't look. You might lose your lunch!

DEENA. Oh, it's the "porcupine head." If she knows what's good for her, she better stay away from Michael. And she better stay away from me.

AMY. Hey, porcupine! Check your needles lately?

JO-LETTE. Why doesn't she just do what we told her to do…and go *kill* herself!

DARIUS. Nobody would miss her.

DEENA. What was with you talking to her, Michael, when you know I can't stand her?

JO-LETTE. Nobody can.

MICHAEL T. I wasn't talking to her! She's always coming on to me. I hate it. Don't forget, I was the one who put the open ketchup packs on the chair before she sat down.

(ALL laugh.)

AMY. Her pants were *nasty* all day, and nobody told her!

DARIUS. Wait here. I'll go get my car...pick you up in a minute. We can get to her again before the bus does.

(Exit DARIUS.)

DEENA. I've got a water bottle to throw at her.

AMY. Me, too.

JO-LETTE. Make sure you take the lids off this time. It's more fun when she's soaked.

(ALL laugh.)

MICHAEL T. She won't know what hit her. Wish I had that cup of ice I just threw away.

DEENA. I hope she falls like she did the last time I got her.

AMY. She limped for a week!

JO-LETTE. Did you know she brought her mom in to talk to Principal Aubrey this morning?

DEENA. Sandy works in the office in the morning and told us. Even the counselor was there.

MICHAEL T. I'm not surprised. She's dumber than I thought she was.

JO-LETTE. That was a stupid thing to do.

DEENA. Everybody knows Mr. Aubrey and Counselor Roth hate her too.

AMY. She just needs to do us all a favor and go *die*.

DEENA. I'm sure I can help her along the way if she crosses me one more time.

MICHAEL T. Here he comes now. It's Darius. Hurry up if we want to get to her before she gets on the bus.

JO-LETTE. Get the bottles unscrewed! Let's go!

DEENA. Quick, quick. Let's get in the car! Her bus is coming.

(ALL exit, laughing. LIGHTS out.

LIGHTS up. Enter DARIUS and AMY from R, MICHAEL T., DEENA and JO-LETTE from L.)

DARIUS. Hey, guys! No need to worry about yesterday on the way home. My car started right up this morning.

JO-LETTE. Didn't you two hear?

DARIUS. Hear what?

DEENA. Where have you been all morning? It's all over the news.

AMY. What's all over the news?

MICHAEL T. It's HER. She finally did it.

DARIUS. What'd she do?

AMY. Don't tell me. She went home and threw her clothes in the dryer.

(AMY and DARIUS laugh.)

DARIUS. It was so *sick* the way she got hit. Whack! Splat! Splat!

AMY. We soaked her!

(AMY and DARIUS laugh.)

JO-LETTE. She went home yesterday afternoon…

DEENA. …and hanged herself from the back porch.

(LIGHTS out.)

END OF PLAY

Here Be Dragons

By Doug Cooney

CHARACTERS

BOOPIE.. 14, an athletic boy
CASSIE .... 12 to 14, a tall, popular girl
SIMON .... 12 to 13, a short, brainy boy
TYRANNOSAURUS.. a dinosaur
APATOSAURUS.. a dinosaur
VELOCIRAPTOR... a dinosaur

NOTE: The three middle-school students are not friends. The dinosaurs can be portrayed by average kids in street clothes, using posture and attitude.

SETTING AND TIME: A natural history museum. The present.

ACKNOWLEDGMENTS: Special thanks to Elizabeth Wong and Christian Lebano.

(Three DINOSAURS are exhibited: a TYRANNOSAUR-US, an APATOSAURUS and a VELOCIRAPTOR. Three middle-school STUDENTS visit the exhibit on a field trip.)

BOOPIE. "Here Be Dragons"? Stupid title. These aren't dragons. They're *dinosaurs.*

SIMON *(you idiot—)*. What it means is—back in medieval days, maps marked the unknown, dangerous territory "here be dragons."

CASSIE. But that's medieval. Dinosaurs are prehistoric.

BOOPIE *(to SIMON, re: short and brainy)*. Is this some *hobbit* thing?

SIMON. I didn't name the stinkin' exhibit. Mr. Miyake says dinosaurs are closer to birds than to dragons anyway…

BOOPIE *(oh, sure)*. "Birds," right. Brainiac.

CASSIE. Loser.

SIMON *(calling them both out)*. *Hey!* Name-calling! I'm telling Mr. Miyake.

CASSIE *(ditto)*. Tattletale! I'm telling Mr. Miyake.

BOOPIE *(ditto)*. I hear threats! I'm telling Miyake.

SIMON, CASSIE & BOOPIE *(you're a—)*. —*Bully.*

(A brief stalemate.)

SIMON *(sulking, re: VELOCIRAPTOR)*. If I was this dinosaur, I'd tear you up!

BOOPIE *(re: TYRANNOSAURUS)*. No—because I'd be *this* dinosaur and I'd tear *you* up!

CASSIE. You're both wrong. Dinosaurs would have already eaten us all. We'd be in their intestines, turning into dinosaur poop.

BOOPIE *(laughing)*. Poop.

SIMON. I'm telling Mr. Miyake. You said "poop."

CASSIE *(in his face)*. Oh—poop, poop, poop. I hate being stuck in Mr. Miyake's buddy system. This alphabetical order sucks! I'd be having much more fun if I was with my friends.

SIMON. Me too.

CASSIE. Oh, really? You have friends? *(That was mean. Simon has no friends.)*

BOOPIE *(to CASSIE)*. You don't have friends. Not really.

CASSIE. What is *that* supposed to mean?

BOOPIE *(doesn't respond. He reads the plaque below the T-Rex)*. "Tyrannosaurus. 'Tyrant Lizard.' Late Cretaceous Period. 68-65 million years ago." Cool. *(He roars.)*

CASSIE *(everything you do annoys me)*. Ugh.

(The STUDENTS don't hear—but the DINOSAURS speak. They look ferocious in posture and demeanor—but, unexpectedly, they are surprisingly pleasant and polite, almost shy, when they speak.)

TYRANNOSAURUS. Did you hear that? That sounds nothing like me.

APATOSAURUS. Hush. They'll hear you.

VELOCIRAPTOR. And it's not polite to eavesdrop.

TYRANNOSAURUS. All we ever do is eavesdrop.

SIMON *(reads the VELOCIRAPTOR's plaque)*. "Velociraptor. 'Swift Predator.'" Okay, that's me. "Late Cretaceous Period. 84-80 million years ago."

VELOCIRAPTOR *(to DINOSAURS, re: SIMON)*. Smart kid, isn't he? I imagine he's awfully bright.

TYRANNOSAURUS. Frankly, I could eat these smart kids in one bite. In my day, I would have mowed through them like McNuggets.

APATOSAURUS. Oh, what a monster you were. All that's over now...

BOOPIE *(re: APATOSAURUS)*. And that Brontosaurus is you, Cassie. You know why?

CASSIE. It's not Brontosaurus, Lizard Brains. It's "Apatosaurus."

BOOPIE. You wanna know why, hunh? You wanna know why?...

CASSIE *(re: APATOSAURUS, reading)*. "'Deceptive Lizard.' Late *Jurassic* Period, 156-144 million years ago." Whoa. *Old.*

BOOPIE. —'Cause you're both "Too Tall." It's the "Too Tall" family!

CASSIE. Ha-ha, funny. So funny I forgot to laugh.

BOOPIE *(advancing like a DINOSAUR)*. Tooo Taalllllll. Hey, Tooooo Taaaaalllll.

CASSIE. Cut it out.

VELOCIRAPTOR *(to APATOSAURUS)*. I don't mean to eavesdrop—

APATOSAURUS. —Neither do I, but unfortunately...

VELOCIRAPTOR. —Was he being "nice" or was he being "mean?"...

APATOSAURUS. —I think "nice" maybe...

BOOPIE. You're so tall, you tripped in Texas, skinned your knee in Nebraska and hit your head on the North Pole.

(The DINOSAURS register "oooh!" and "awww!" to the zingers, like spectators at a tennis match.)

APATOSAURUS *(to VELOCIRAPTOR)*. —Correction, make that "mean."

BOOPIE. Hey, Too Tall! Didn't your mama tell you not to be *too long*?

CASSIE. Your jokes are so stupid...

APATOSAURUS *(to VELOCIRAPTOR)*. —And rather dull.

SIMON *(reacts to BOOPIE's behavior. To CASSIE)*. Just ignore him. He's only trying to get your attention...

BOOPIE *(to CASSIE, ignoring SIMON)*. I'm glad you're too tall. It gives me more of you to dislike...

SIMON. —It's so obvious that he *likes* you.

CASSIE. Him? Me? *Gross*, he does *not*!

SIMON. I've seen it before. *(To BOOPIE.)* Bring it on, Boopie. No short jokes for me?

BOOPIE. I'm just gettin' started, shrimp. You're so short...

SIMON. —My brains are in my butt, right? Funny.

(The DINOSAURS cluck like hens.)

BOOPIE. No—I was gonna say—"You're so short—"

SIMON. —My driver's license photo is head to toe. Oh, funny...

BOOPIE. —Are you making fun of me, runt?

SIMON. "Shrimp." "Runt." Ouch. A kid called me "dwarf" at my old school. Know what happened to him?

BOOPIE. What?

SIMON. The brain melt.

CASSIE *(gasps with recognition)*. "The brain melt?" Did you go to Emerson?

SIMON. Emerson Middle.

CASSIE. The "brain melt" kid?! You're famous! *(To BOOPIE, genuine.)* Sally, my cousin at Emerson, told me this brain melt kid reads your personality in thirty seconds and then he *melts your brain.*

BOOPIE. Cannot.

SIMON. Can so.

BOOPIE. Cannot.

SIMON. Can *do*. Try me.

CASSIE. Don't mess with him, Boopie! Sally says your brain drips out your ears!

BOOPIE. Like I'm scared. *(To SIMON, bring it on.)* Hello, Shrimp! Runt! Dwarf!

SIMON. I have accessed your brain. Set systems on "melt."

BOOPIE & TYRANNOSAURUS. What's he doing?

APATOSAURUS. I'm scared.

VELOCIRAPTOR. These kids are monstrous!

SIMON *(initiates the brain melt. To BOOPIE, diagnostic)*. Boopie: a big kid for seventh grade—so I'm guessing he was held back a year. Either held back or *flunked*.

BOOPIE *(direct hit)*. *Whoa! Hey!!*

SIMON *(full brain melt)*. His vocabulary is limited, his jokes are dumb—and his name is a playground name, so *his parents probably got divorced* when he was way-little...

BOOPIE *(wounded)*. —What?! Who told?

SIMON. —And his mom or grandparent was distracted or busy or working two jobs and didn't read enough to him...

BOOPIE. —Cut it out!...

SIMON. —And dropped him in front of a television and that's how he developed such a lame personality.

BOOPIE. Stop it! Stop! Make him stop! *Heeeey! (A pause. He is clearly hurt.)* That wasn't nice. That was *mean*.

SIMON. You were mean.

BOOPIE. I was *joking*! *You* were mean!

CASSIE. You're such a bully, Simon.

SIMON. I'm a little guy! I'm not the bully here! You are!

CASSIE. Me?! What did I do?!

SIMON. I sat next to you on the bus and you got up and walked away.

CASSIE. That doesn't make me a bully. What is *your* problem? I don't have to sit with you if I don't want.

SIMON. No. But then I was sitting with your friends—and you made them get up and go sit with you too.

CASSIE. You're sick or something. That's all in your head. I don't remember that.

BOOPIE *(to CASSIE)*. You've done that to me. You and your friends...

CASSIE *(to BOOPIE)*. How can you say that? I thought you "liked" me!

BOOPIE. —You all ditched me in the cafeteria that one time. And then you were all whispering about me. I felt weird all day.

CASSIE. The two of you are ganging up on me! I'm telling Mr. Miyake.

BOOPIE. You're the one who gangs up.

SIMON. Yeah, go back to your supposed friends.

CASSIE. They *are* my friends!

SIMON. You wouldn't say that if you knew what they say behind your back. Right, Boopie?

BOOPIE. Right.

CASSIE *(to SIMON)*. Don't pull your "brain melt" on me!

BOOPIE *(fake concern)*. What, are you going to cry? Omigosh, I think she's gonna cry.

SIMON. Go on and cry, crybaby. Crybaby-bully!

CASSIE. I'm not the bully; you are!

SIMON *(to CASSIE)*. No you are!

BOOPIE *(to SIMON)*. No you are!

CASSIE *(to BOOPIE)*. No you are!

BOOPIE *(to CASSIE)*. No—you are!

SIMON *(louder, to CASSIE)*. Yeah, YOU ARE!

CASSIE *(louder still, to BOOPIE)*. NO! YOU ARE!!

(It builds until...a dinosaur ROAR, loud, long, ferocious. [If possible, an authentic sound cue, not a kid-generated noise.] The STUDENTS scream, trembling with fear.)

BOOPIE. *Dinosaurs!*

SIMON. We're poop! We're poop! We're...

ALL THREE KIDS. —Dinosaur poop!

(LIGHTS shift: mystical, creepy, prehistoric. The ROARING fades into the distance. The DINOSAURS present

themselves. Again, they appear ferocious—but are surprisingly gentle.)

TYRANNOSAURUS. Hey—hush now. Settle down.

VELOCIRAPTOR. We don't mean any harm.

APATOSAURUS. Gosh, sorry if that got too loud, but we had to get your attention. And you were making such a racket!

VELOCIRAPTOR. Wow. You kids are vicious! It never lets up!

TYRANNOSAURUS. It's fascinating, really. Are you always at each other's throats?

BOOPIE. Not always. Well…

CASSIE. —It happens…

SIMON. —Maybe. Mostly—

CASSIE *(insert the appropriate year)*. —It *is* seventh grade…

VELOCIRAPTOR. Wowie-wow-wow. I thought the Cretaceous Period was bad—but seventh grade is ferocious!

CASSIE. It's not so bad. High school is worse.

APATOSAURUS. Worse like the Jurassic Period—?

TYRANNOSAURUS *(appreciative)*. *Whoa!*…

ALL THREE DINOSAURS. —*Here Be Dragons.*

SIMON. We're not dragons.

BOOPIE *(to DINOSAURS)*. *You're* the dragons.

VELOCIRAPTOR *(you idiot)*. No, we're not. We're dinosaurs.

TYRANNOSAURUS. Dinosaurs had it rough—but nothing like middle school. You dragons are so awful to each other.

APATOSAURUS. I wonder if middle school turns you into a dragon—or turning into a dragon means you're in middle school…

CASSIE. Wait a minute. We're just kids being kids! We're not *dragons*! You guys actually *ate* each other.

TYRANNOSAURUS. Only because we were hungry!

APATOSAURUS. Excuse me! I was an herbivore. Strictly green. But I will say—if I ran into a carnivore and he wasn't hungry, he could be quite pleasant and polite. Unless he was hungry.

VELOCIRAPTOR. Even then it was only claws and teeth! Never words or spite!

APATOSAURUS. —Or whispering!—or insults—!

TYRANNOSAURUS. —Or names! Omigosh, the *names!* You dragons are awesome! *(A beat, then...)* Teach us to be like you!

APATOSAURUS. No-no-no, it's too late for that. Our time has passed...

VELOCIRAPTOR. And our brains were the size of peanuts! We could never have come up with really mean things to say...

APATOSAURUS. —Right. Certainly not like dragons. I can't say I'd want to be a dragon. They're so solitary and unhappy and they never have any friends, not really.

VELOCIRAPTOR. Who could they trust?

SIMON. Hold up! Wrong! We're not dragons; we're kids!

TYRANNOSAURUS. But you act like dragons.

CASSIE. That's only to protect ourselves!—

APATOSAURUS. —Protect from what?—

CASSIE. —From other kids!

BOOPIE. It gets kinda dog-eat-dog. Kinda kid-eat-kid.

SIMON. And some kids are *mean.*

BOOPIE *(meaning SIMON).* I know a few.

SIMON. *Hey!*

CASSIE. We're not bullies! We're protecting ourselves! You know! You were dinosaur-eat-dinosaur. You protected yourselves!

TYRANNOSAURUS. I never actually protected myself. Maybe I'm old school but it was always easier just to eat 'em than to talk about it.

APATOSAURUS *(to TYRANNOSAURUS)*. Oh, listen to you. You protected yourself! You had that Tyrannosaurus Walk!

TYRANNOSAURUS. Oh, yeaaaaah, remember that?! *(To BOOPIE.)* Head up, shoulders back, purpose, somewhere to go. Nobody messes with the Tyrannosaurus Walk!

APATOSAURUS *(to CASSIE)*. I was lucky. I was bigger than most back then, still am. An Apatosaurus didn't move fast but was always tall enough to see trouble coming and sound the alarm—or avoid it!

VELOCIRAPTOR *(to SIMON)*. Velociraptors—we worked in a pack, stuck together like a team. That way we had each other's back. No one gets left behind. And if you got camouflage, use it. Lay low.

APATOSAURUS. A fight was always the least original response to a fight when you could hide back, stay quiet or throw a distraction.

TYRANNOSAURUS. You should never fight when you can't win the fight.

CASSIE. But see—we're the same way! We're just protecting ourselves!

BOOPIE. Sometimes you attack to let them know you protect yourself...

VELOCIRAPTOR. —Attack-protect, protect-attack, they look the same to me!

APATOSAURUS. I never noticed what a vicious cycle it can be.

TYRANNOSAURUS. But you're protecting yourselves. You're asking for trouble! Use your brains!

APATOSAURUS. We never had brains! We were never so smart...

VELOCIRAPTOR. —Never so mean…

TYRANNOSAURUS. —We were just hungry. Trying to survive. You dragons…

APATOSAURUS. It's so funny! All this time, I thought they had *evolved*!

(The DINOSAURS LAUGH. It grows into a low RUMBLE—another ROAR, traveling into the distance. LIGHTS shift; the DINOSAURS freeze. The STUDENTS stand at the exhibit.)

BOOPIE. What just happened?

CASSIE. They called us dragons.

SIMON. I never thought of myself as a dragon before.

BOOPIE. What? You thought you were a hobbit?

SIMON. *Hey!*

CASSIE. That name-calling is what they were talking about. They call us "dragons"—but middle school is *nothing* like high school. I don't want to think about high school; I don't want it to be dangerous —I want it to be fun…

BOOPIE. —But it *is* unknown territory. I worry too…

SIMON. I have nightmares about high school.

CASSIE. Me too.

BOOPIE. Me three.

ALL THREE KIDS *(re: high school)*. *There Be Dragons.*

SIMON. So what can we do? How do we protect ourselves?

BOOPIE. Either stick together—or turn into dragons. *(He roars again.)* That's my plan.

CASSIE. I don't wanna be a dragon. I got a brain. I want to evolve.

BOOPIE *(to Simon)*. Hey, Brain Melt. You should practice that Tyrannosaurus Walk. You're gonna need it. Head up, shoulders back, walk with purpose. Don't mess with me, *I am Brain Melt!*

CASSIE. Enough with the name-calling.

BOOPIE. What—? You gonna tell?

CASSIE. Maybe. The Apatosaurus kept an eye out and sounded the alarm.

SIMON. Velociraptors stayed in a pack. They had each other's back.

CASSIE. We could do that. We could watch out for each other…

BOOPIE. —We could, maybe. I'd be okay with that. The three of us?

SIMON. No deal.

CASSIE. What's the matter?

BOOPIE. Yeah, what's your problem, Frodo?

SIMON *(considers them before he speaks. To CASSIE)*. Can I trust you?

CASSIE *(to BOOPIE)*. Can I trust you?

BOOPIE *(to SIMON)*. Can I trust you?

SIMON *(to BOOPIE)*. Can I trust you?

CASSIE *(to SIMON)*. Can I trust you?

BOOPIE *(to CASSIE)*. Can I trust you?

(A low, distant dinosaur ROAR.)

END OF PLAY

Mindless, Drooling, Teenage Zombie Bullies

By Brian Guehring

This script was inspired by an improvisation about homophobia and bullying by Nik Whitcomb, Colleen Kilcoyne, Amanda Harris, Sami Mines, Anne Johnson, Dan Burgdorf and the teen company of Pride Players 12 at the Omaha Theater Company.

CHARACTERS

COLLEEN .... a shy high-school student who faces homophobia at her school

DAN .... Colleen's best friend with a very dry sense of humor and a brilliant mind for chemistry

LEILANI .... Colleen's confident teen activist girlfriend (who attends Central High School)

NIK .... a homophobic athletic boy at East High

SAMI .... Nik's girlfriend

AMANDA .... Sami's friend

MS. JOHNSON .... Colleen's chemistry teacher

ZOMBIE TEENS .... East High students affected by the botched chemistry experiment

GSA TEENS .... members of Central High GSA who host the Pride Party

SETTING AND TIME: East High School chemistry class; Colleen's home; Central High's Pride Party. Now.

Scene 1: Chemistry Class

(MS. JOHNSON is supervising COLLEEN, DAN, SAMI, NIK, AMANDA and other STUDENTS working on experiments in chemistry lab.)

MS. JOHNSON. OK, class, you should be finishing up the experiment and writing down your measurements and observations. We start cleaning up in five minutes.

NIK. Dude, this chem lab is so gay.

(COLLEEN winces.)

MS. JOHNSON. Let's focus, class.

DAN. Aren't you done, Colleen?

(SAMI smiles at COLLEEN, who smiles back. NIK then whispers to SAMI who starts ignoring COLLEEN.)

COLLEEN. No, Dan. I'm having a hard time concentrating. *(She notices NIK then whispering to AMANDA, pointing at COLLEEN and laughing.)*

DAN. I finished ten minutes ago.

AMANDA *(comes to COLLEEN's table on her way to put away her equipment).* So is the rumor true, Colleen?

COLLEEN. What?

AMANDA. That you are a big jolly lesbian. *(COLLEEN doesn't answer.)* OMG, you are! *(She goes back to her table and tells SAMI.)*

DAN. What's going on?

COLLEEN. Nik saw me last night at a coffee shop with a girl from Central. And he's telling everyone that I'm gay.

DAN. You told Nik you were gay?

COLLEEN. Of course I didn't.

DAN. Well...ummm...maybe you should just ignore him.

COLLEEN. But now he's telling everyone. It's like everything that comes out of his mouth makes more people hate me.

(NIK and other chemistry STUDENTS point to COLLEEN and laugh.)

DAN. Nik is a bully and has always been a bully. There is nothing we can do to make him nice.

COLLEEN. You could stand up to him and help me out.

DAN. Oh, yeah, a nerdy chemistry geek can stop the football player from picking on you. Actually… *(He starts a new experiment.)*

COLLEEN. What are you doing now, then?

DAN. I have an idea that I want to test out. A new experiment.

COLLEEN. Is that safe?

DAN. Trust me. I'm going to MIT as a chem major. I know what I'm doing.

(NIK starts texting on his phone. COLLEEN's phone buzzes. She picks it up.)

COLLEEN. Great, now he's texting me insults, too.

(NIK starts laughing and AMANDA joins in.)

MS. JOHNSON. No cell phones in class, Colleen. Bring me your phone.

(COLLEEN walks to front of class.)

NIK *(as if he is sneezing)*. Aahhhh… Dyke.

(NIK and CLASS laugh as COLLEEN hands over phone.)

COLLEEN. Did you hear that, Ms. Johnson?

NIK. I just sneezed.

MS. JOHNSON. Colleen, focus on your schoolwork in school, not your personal life.

COLLEEN *(returns to her table)*. Even the teachers won't help me.

DAN. Teens say that stuff all the time, the teachers have become numb to it. There is nothing anyone can do. Just don't bring attention to yourself and hope it goes away.

(NIK approaches DAN and COLLEEN's table. DAN and COLLEEN are on one side of the table and the rest of the CLASS is on the other side.)

NIK. Why don't you just transfer to another school, freak?

(NIK spits at COLLEEN. DAN and COLLEEN hold up folders to protect themselves, and the spit lands in DAN's experiment. SOUND of explosion. The entire CLASS except for DAN and COLLEEN have been sprayed by the chemical explosion and react.)

MS. JOHNSON *(wiping off chemicals from her face)*. What just happened?

DAN *(trying to clean up)*. Nik just spit into my experiment.

SAMI. Which exploded all over us!

MS. JOHNSON. What were you doing?

DAN. I was trying something new…

MS. JOHNSON. Dan, I will deal with you later! Quickly—everyone out of the room!

(CLASS leaves room, coughing and looking ill.)

COLLEEN. What just happened?

DAN. A fascinatingly unexpected chemistry reaction. I did not think that human saliva could cause my experiment to explode like that.

COLLEEN. What were you working on, Dan?

DAN. A little chemical formula to stimulate the prefrontal cortex.

COLLEEN. What?

DAN. The part of your brain responsible for empathy, judgment and impulse control. I was planning to test it on rats first. This will be much more interesting.

COLLEEN. Thank goodness it didn't spray on us.

DAN. I wonder if it will take long to notice any changes in the subjects.

(Ominous SOUND of moaning.)

COLLEEN. I'm going to talk to Sami. See if she'll help me with Nik.

COLLEEN *(approaches SAMI)*. Sami, can I talk to you? *(SAMI moans.)* OK, um...look I know Nik is your boyfriend. But he's really harassing me, and I was hoping since we've known each other since kindergarten you could talk to him. *(SAMI moans, stares at COLLEEN.)*

DAN. Colleen, maybe we should get out of here.

COLLEEN. Please, Sami. I could use some support.

DAN. Now is not a good time, Colleen. I think we should leave. Now.

(MOANING gets louder as DAN pulls a dejected COLLEEN out.)

Scene 2: Colleen's Home

(COLLEEN is getting ready for a party. DAN knocks.)

COLLEEN *(opens the door)*. Hey.

DAN. Hey. I was just checking to see how you are doing.

COLLEEN. Fine. I guess.

DAN. Wow. You're all dressed up. Where are you going tonight?

COLLEEN. I'm going to a party at Central High School with Leilani.

DAN. What kinda party?

COLLEEN. They are having a Pride Party. It's a safe space for all kids, whether they're straight or gay.

DAN. That's cool. So, what's the new girlfriend like?

COLLEEN. She's not a girlfriend…yet. She's just a girl who's a friend. But she's amazing and beautiful. She is so confident and stands up for what she believes in. A real fighter, you know?

DAN. That's cool. It'll also be good to get away from the jerks at our school.

COLLEEN. Yeah, I'm not looking forward to Monday.

DAN. I'm sure this whole thing will just blow over.

(Doorbell RINGS.)

COLLEEN. That must be Leilani.

(COLLEEN crosses to the door and opens it as an ashen SAMI slowly comes in.)

DAN. Sami, what are you doing here?

SAMI *(grunting)*. Lesbo!

COLLEEN *(backing up)*. Sami, it's me. I'm still the same girl I was when we were in Girl Scouts together.

SAMI *(coming toward COLLEEN slowly and menacingly)*. Kill!

(SAMI gets her arms up to COLLEEN's neck. DAN rushes and pushes SAMI away. SAMI starts reaching for DAN. COLLEEN backs up toward window. NIK's arm reaches through window to sound of breaking glass and grabs a terrified COLLEEN. LEILANI bursts in.)

LEILANI. GET AWAY FROM MY DATE! *(She pushes down the window, trapping NIK's arm.)*

COLLEEN. Thank you, Leilani.

DAN *(still holding back struggling SAMI)*. You must be the new girlfriend. I'm Dan.

LEILANI. Nice to meet you, but WHAT'S GOING ON HERE?!!

DAN *(still holding back a struggling SAMI)*. Colleen was outed at school and reaction hasn't been all positive.

LEILANI. We need to get out of here! NOW!

COLLEEN. Where are we going to go?

LEILANI. To the Pride Party! There's safety in numbers! LET'S GO! NOW!!

(LEILANI, DAN and COLLEEN exit as SAMI and NIK slowly follow.)

Scene 3: Central High School Pride Party

(COLLEEN, LEILANI and DAN are running to the dance.)

COLLEEN. Nobody is here yet.

LEILANI. We're early.

COLLEEN. I can't believe Sami and Nik attacked me in my own home.

LEILANI. Is everyone in your school a mindless, angry homophobe?

DAN. They're like zombies…oh, no.

COLLEEN. Zombies? What?

DAN. The chemical contamination…by adding Nik's homophobic DNA it seems to have altered the expected outcome of the experiment. Rather than increasing the subjects' overall empathy, maybe it made them empathize with Nik's homophobic views.

COLLEEN. What did you do?

LEILANI. Your friend created a horde of mindless, drooling, homophobic teenage zombies.

(NIK, AMANDA and SAMI slowly enter party.)

DAN. Since my chemical experiment was contaminated, *technically* I just *contributed* to the creation of these zombies.

COLLEEN. You created a mob of mindless, homophobic teenage zombies.

DAN. Again, technically, Nik already was homophobic. The experiment just made his homophobia even more contagious. And the chemical just erased their impulse control and made them homicidal.

LEILANI. YOU TURNED YOUR ENTIRE SCHOOL INTO HOMOPHOBIC, HOMICIDAL ZOMBIES!

DAN. Once again, technically, I only created a small group. Just our chemistry class. There weren't that many people in chem. Unless…

COLLEEN. Unless what?

DAN. Unless it is contagious.

(More ZOMBIE TEENS enter the party and slowly start toward the unaware COLLEEN, DAN and LEILANI.)

LEILANI. The homophobia zombie disease is contagious? How could it be passed from one teen to another, Dan?

DAN. Probably through saliva…

LEILANI. So all it would take to spread this disease is for them to share a drink or for these hormonal teens to kiss another teen?

DAN. I guess. Hmmmm…this probably isn't good.

LEILANI. We have an epidemic!

COLLEEN. We have to get out of here!

(ZOMBIES moan as they get closer.)

LEILANI. Too late. They crashed the party. *(She starts pushing down the first group who fall easily. The ZOMBIES just keep walking over the prone ZOMBIES, though.)*

COLLEEN. What are we going to do? *(MS. JOHNSON appears with her back to the audience.)* Hey, look: there's Ms. Johnson. Maybe she can help.

DAN. Wait—what is she even doing here?

(COLLEEN, DAN and LEILANI approach MS. JOHN-SON.)

COLLEEN. Ms. Johnson, I am so glad you are here!

(MS. JOHNSON turns around. She is ashen-faced and drooling. She sees COLLEEN and DAN and moans angrily. COLLEEN, LEILANI and DAN quickly retreat to center stage.)

DAN. OK, she still seems angry about the explosion.

COLLEEN. Dan, how can we stop these zombies?

DAN. I don't know!

LEILANI. Maybe if you spent more time standing up for your friend and less time in your crazy chemistry land, we wouldn't have had this problem!!

DAN. I'M SORRY!

(ZOMBIES are getting closer. More TEENS arrive.)

COLLEEN. More zombies are arriving?

LEILANI. No, these are my friends! The ones who helped me put together this Pride Party.

GSA TEEN 1. Leilani, are you all right?

LEILANI. No, we need help!

(The GSA TEENS immediately surround LEILANI, COLLEEN and DAN, then start MUSIC.)

DAN. What are they doing?! Now is not the time to start dancing.

GSA TEEN 3. Never underestimate the power of dance.

(SONG starts. GSA TEENS start grabbing ZOMBIES and dancing.)

GSA TEEN 1. Leave them alone. They aren't hurting you.

GSA TEEN 2. Wouldn't you rather have fun?

GSA TEEN 3. Come on! Get to know us! We're not that different from you.

(Dancing continues until ZOMBIES collapse, exhausted.)

COLLEEN. OK, the zombies are exhausted. Let's get out of here.

(SAMI, AMANDA and ZOMBIES slowly get up, shaking their heads. NIK is still down.)

SAMI. What's going on?

AMANDA. Where are we?

GSA TEEN 1. You're at the Central High School Pride Party.

ZOMBIE TEEN 1 *(grunting)*. Looks fun.

(ZOMBIES turn back into regular TEENS and join party.)

COLLEEN. What just happened? Why aren't they attacking us anymore? Why didn't the Central High kids become zombies?

DAN. The Central High teens obviously have been inoculated from the contagious homophobia.

LEILANI. By education.

DAN. And their open minds and positive words combined with the kinesthetic dance experience, accompanying swapping of sweat and euphoria created by having fun, counteracted my chemical reaction. This increased the activity in their prefrontal cortex causing more empathy. Maybe if I try a new formula…

LEILANI. NO!

NIK *(wakes up and grabs COLLEEN)*. Freak!

DAN. Get away from her!

(DAN pushes him away. NIK grunts but the GSA TEENS surround him and start pushing him out of the party.)

GSA TEEN 1. Get out of here, you bully!

GSA TEEN 2. We don't put up with that here.

(NIK is outnumbered, and pushed into room.)

DAN. They just locked Nik in the closet. Nice.

COLLEEN. Leilani, how did you get so many cool people at Central High School?

LEILANI. We started a GSA.

DAN. A what?

LEILANI. A Gay Straight Alliance. We work together to make school safe for all students.

DAN. And you throw killer parties… Well maybe killer is the wrong adjective to use…

COLLEEN. We should start a GSA at East High School.

LEILANI. Yep. Just like homophobia is contagious, so is standing up for equality.

COLLEEN. Our school needs that.

LEILANI. A GSA won't stop all homophobic bullying, but it will help. And studies have shown that having a GSA definitely eliminates all violent, homophobic zombie attacks.[1]

COLLEEN. Will you help me start one at East High, Dan? I'm tired of facing all this mindless bullying all by myself. Sometimes I feel so alone in this.

DAN. I promise.

(A new SONG starts.)

LEILANI. Then it sounds like we have something to celebrate!

(Entire CAST starts to dance again.)

END OF PLAY

[1] For more information about starting a GSA or statistics from the latest survey about safety in schools for LGBT students, go to www.GLSEN.org

The New Kid

By Richard Dresser

CHARACTERS

MAX................................a 12-year-old (played by an adult)
KIRK ....a 12-year-old (played by an adult)
CONNIE...........................a 12-year-old (played by an adult)
JIM.......................................Max's dad (played by a student)
ANNA .... Max's mom (played by a student)
MIKE...................................Kirk's dad (played by a student)
BONNIE........................... Kirk's mom (played by a student)

SETTING AND TIME: The hallway in a middle school; the living room of Max's house. The present.

Scene 1: The School Hallway

(MAX is headed for the lunchroom with books under his arm. KIRK comes up behind MAX and knocks his books to the floor. KIRK is joined by CONNIE. As MAX bends over to pick up his books, KIRK kicks him in the butt, knocking him to the floor. KIRK and CONNIE laugh. MAX sees who it is. He sighs.)

MAX. What are you doing, Kirk?
KIRK. Taking your lunch money, dick-wad. Let's go! I'm
    hungry!
MAX. This is my money. My mom gave it to me.

CONNIE. Oh, sorry, we won't take it if your mommy gave it to you.

MAX. Really?

KIRK. How did you get to be so stupid, Max? You must really work at it. Now give it up before things get ugly.

(MAX reluctantly gives them his lunch money as the school BELL RINGS. They scatter.)

Scene 2: Max's House

(JIM, MAX's dad, is reading the paper. ANNA, MAX's mom, is concerned.)

ANNA. He's just not himself.

JIM *(not paying attention)*. Then who is he? Anyone we know?

ANNA. Jim, he's a very unhappy boy.

JIM *(puts down paper)*. Look, I know this move has not been easy for any of us. But we have great jobs, a great house, a great dog, a great neighborhood, a great school—

ANNA. I'm not so sure about that school. *(Calls.)* Max!

MAX *(enters in his pajamas)*. What did I do?

ANNA. Nothing, honey. We just want to make sure everything is okay.

MAX. Yeah, everything's great. Can we move?

JIM. Why do you want to move?

MAX. At my old school I had friends. And the kids weren't a bunch of dorks.

ANNA. Can we find a nicer word?

MAX. Scuzzballs?

ANNA. Keep going.

MAX. Ignoramuses?

ANNA. All right, why are these kids ignoramuses?

MAX. Maybe they had a bad childhood?

JIM. Max. What happened?

MAX. They took my lunch money.

ANNA. That's it. I'm going to call the principal.

MAX. Don't do that. Please, Mom?

JIM. Your mother is wonderful in these situations. She'll know exactly what to say.

MAX. It's only going to make it worse!

ANNA. Honey, let us take care of it. There's no reason a child should be afraid to go to school.

(MAX exits.)

JIM. So what are you going to say to the principal, Anna?

ANNA. I don't have any idea.

JIM. Maybe we should just let it work itself out.

ANNA. It's already out of hand! Stealing his money? We have to *do something*!

Scene 3: The School Hallway

(MAX sees KIRK and CONNIE and moves faster.)

KIRK. Hang on, pal. Can I borrow your phone?

MAX. How come?

KIRK. I forgot mine and I have to call home. C'mon, what are friends for?

MAX *(hands him the phone)*. Okay, just for one quick call.

CONNIE. Wow, my cat is smarter than you, Max. And my cat is not that smart.

(KIRK and CONNIE start off laughing.)

MAX. Hey, give me back my phone!

KIRK. Oh, we'll give it back.

CONNIE. Just as soon as we tell the rest of the school what you really think of them!

MAX. Don't do that! *Please?*

(The school BELL RINGS. They scatter.)

Scene 4: Max's House

(JIM is reading the paper. ANNA comes in, anxious.)

ANNA. Should we be giving them dinner? Or drinks? Or *something*?

JIM. Anna, these are not our friends.

ANNA. Well, they might be. I mean you never know, right?

JIM. Sometimes you know.

(Doorbell. JIM opens the door on MIKE and BONNIE, KIRK's parents.)

JIM. Oh, hello. I'm Jim…this is my wife…

ANNA. Anna! Hi!

MIKE. I'm Mike.

BONNIE. Bonnie.

JIM. Have a seat. Thanks for coming over.

BONNIE. Thanks for asking us. I mean, if there's a problem…

ANNA. Does anyone want anything?

MIKE. I'll have a cheeseburger. Medium rare, onion rings, a beer. Can you do that?

ANNA. Oh…all right…

MIKE. Hey, I'm kidding. Everyone's so jumpy, let's just deal with this thing, whatever it is.

JIM. Thanks, Mike. The problem is—

ANNA. Maybe it's more of a misunderstanding...

JIM. The *problem* is, your son Kirk *facebooked* half the school pretending to be our son Max. And he basically trashed them with some extremely vulgar language. So now all the other students think Max is a pretty awful person.

ANNA. And they don't even *know* Max because we're new in town. This has not been easy.

BONNIE. Well I'm just flabbergasted. Mike?

MIKE. Look at this face. This is the face of a man who is flabbergasted.

BONNIE. Kirkie is the sweetest little boy. We've never ever had a problem.

MIKE. I have no issues with Kirk anymore. I draw the line and he does not dare cross it. With lots of parents there are no consequences. I am all about consequences.

BONNIE. Honestly, Kirk does struggle a bit in school because of his learning disability—

MIKE. Right, a "learning disability" called L-A-Z-Y. I told him he gets his act together or I yank his ass out of seventh grade and personally homeschool him. Nobody wants that.

BONNIE. No, they don't, Mike.

ANNA. I'm sure he's a lovely boy.

MIKE. You want to see what a great kid he is? He's waiting in the car. Go get him, Bonnie.

BONNIE. Really? I don't know—

MIKE. What, am I talking to myself? *Move!*

(BONNIE exits.)

MIKE *(cont'd)*. So what do you do, Jim?

JIM. I'm a classics professor over at the college.

MIKE. Nice. Big dollars, summers off, no heavy lifting, huh?

JIM. Well, sort of. And Anna—

ANNA. I edit college textbooks.

MIKE. Oh. So you're smart people, huh?

ANNA. Not really. When something goes wrong in the house, we don't have a clue!

MIKE. I bet.

JIM. What do you do, Mike?

MIKE. I'm a writer.

ANNA. Really? That's wonderful!

MIKE. Yeah, I write my résumé over and over so maybe some punk kid will see fit to hire me for half what I made on my old job.

JIM. That's rough.

MIKE. You got no idea. These days I don't have a dime to give my kid. Bottom line, he's gotta do good in school so he never has to face the crap that is my life. I'm trying to knock some sense into him before it's too late.

(BONNIE and KIRK enter. MIKE throws a few mock punches at KIRK, who's wary around his dad.)

BONNIE. Kirk, this is Mr. and Mrs. Cole.

KIRK. Nice to meet you, Mr. Cole. Mrs. Cole. Is Max around?

ANNA *(calls)*. Max? Can you come and say hello?

MAX *(comes out in his pajamas)*. Hi, everyone!

KIRK. Nice pajamas, Max.

MAX. Thanks.

MIKE. You want some pajamas like that, Kirk? Huh? We'll pick 'em up for Halloween, you'll scare the neighbors.

BONNIE. Mike.

MIKE. I'm kidding! They know I'm kidding, right?

BONNIE. Kirk, is there something you want to say to Max?

KIRK. Maxie, we were just goofing around, kinda giving you a little bit of a hard time. We always do that with new kids.

BONNIE. Hazing?

KIRK. Whatever. Sorry you took it wrong.

MIKE. Sounds like the way *real* guys make friends. Right, Jim?

KIRK. Yeah, like we're not gonna say, "Welcome to our community, Mr. Cole. Won't you please come to our home for cocktails and filet mignon?"

(All the PARENTS laugh.)

MAX. How come you posted all that *facebook* stuff in my name, Kirk?

KIRK. You know what? That was a mistake on Connie's part. How about I come over after school Monday and we post some really funny explanation and make it go away?

ANNA. Does that sound good, Max?

MAX. Okay.

MIKE. There you go. Kids. Am I right, Jim?

JIM. Uh, right.

BONNIE. I'm sorry we got off on the wrong foot. Would you guys like to come over for dinner?

ANNA. That's very sweet, Bonnie. We'd love to!

KIRK. Bye, Max! See you Monday!

(MIKE, BONNIE and KIRK exit.)

JIM. It hurts me to say this but you were right, honey. Sit down and talk to people and you never know what's going to happen.

ANNA. You might even make a few new friends!

Scene 5: The School Hallway

(MAX walks down the hall. KIRK and CONNIE step out of the shadows.)

MAX. Hey, guys, what's happening?

KIRK. Everyone thinks you could make things a whole lot better at this school, Max.

MAX. Yeah? How?

KIRK. If you weren't around anymore.

CONNIE. What kind of little baby goes crying to mommy and daddy? WAAAUGHHHH!

KIRK. We were all set to lay off. But you messed up big time. You give us no choice.

MAX. I thought we were friends.

KIRK. Don't you get it, Max? You don't have any friends.

CONNIE. And you never will. That's a promise.

MAX. Why are you doing this to me?

CONNIE. Why do you think?

MAX. I don't know. But I have my theories.

KIRK. Oh, you have "theories"? Hear that, Connie? He has "theories."

CONNIE. Tell us your "theories," Max.

MAX. I don't think I should.

KIRK. Tell us your "theories," Max. Or we'll throw you out the window.

MAX. Okay. Connie, I watch you with the other girls and it's pretty obvious they don't like you.

CONNIE. What the hell are you talking about?

MAX. You wear all this makeup which is kind of creepy for a twelve-year-old, and it's probably because you're insecure about your weight and your teeth and your neck and stuff. And Kirk's the only boy who talks to you. My theory is you kind of hate yourself. So you have to be better than *someone*, even if it's just the geeky new kid.

(CONNIE turns away.)

KIRK. Hey! You hurt her feelings. What's wrong with you?

MAX. You wanted to hear my theories. It's pretty easy to see why *you're* a bully, Kirk.

KIRK. I don't want to hear it, loser.

CONNIE. How come I had to hear it and you don't, Kirk? That's not fair!

KIRK. Okay, finish your "theory," Max. Then me and Connie are throwing you out the window.

MAX. Kirk, when you drop out of school and go for a job interview and say, "me and Connie," you're not going to get the job. Just like your dad can't get a job.

KIRK. Leave my dad out of this.

MAX. He's part of my theory. He doesn't even give you lunch money. So you steal mine.

KIRK. I take your lunch money because I feel like it and you don't even know how to fight back.

MAX. You're right, I don't. 'Cause my dad doesn't beat me.

KIRK. My dad doesn't beat me!

MAX. I listened before you came into my house. He beats you. He's "all about consequences." And you get so mad you beat on me. Trying to be a big shot like your dad.

KIRK. Shut up, you little freak!

MAX. I got lucky. My parents don't beat me. They talk to me.

CONNIE. And look where it got you.

KIRK. Everyone in school hates you. We made sure of that. So what are you going to do now, Max? Huh?

MAX. I don't know. Maybe I'll just try to talk to the other kids one by one. It won't be so bad. All I need is one friend.

(The school BELL RINGS. MAX moves on to find someone to talk to, full of hope. KIRK and CONNIE are left with each other.)

END OF PLAY

Nobody Nose
(The Trouble I've Seen)

By Barry Kornhauser

Three actors are revealed standing at center, all in a row and facing upstage. After a few moments of stillness, ACTOR 1, who is at the R side of the line, reaches up and touches his/her nose with an index finger. We hear a honk. *(This sound and all the rest to follow may be generated offstage.)* ACTOR 1 lowers his/her hand. A few moments later, ACTOR 2, on the L side, raises his/her index finger to nose, which also gives a honk *(though perhaps of a different pitch).* Then his/her hand is lowered back down. After another moment or two, ACTORS 1 and 2 both poke their noses with their fingers, each generating a simultaneous honk. With that, they both turn around to scrutinize each other. The audience sees what they see, that each has a red clown nose. We also see that the two clearly like what they see in the other, particularly that rosy, round proboscis.

ACTORS 1 and 2 begin to play with their red noses, slowly at first, gently poking and squeezing their own, and, before too long, even each other's nose. They continue to do so with growing enthusiasm, perhaps honking each other's nose with an elbow or knee, touching their noses together, etc., just engaging in all sorts of joyful nose-honking *lazzi.* Their snouts, they think, are very cool, and they enjoy the camaraderie that comes with sharing similar ones.

Eventually, they notice ACTOR 3, who is still facing up-stage. They signal him/her with a honk or two. ACTOR 3 turns around guilelessly, eager to join in the fun. But what's this? He/she does have a clown nose. But it's not a red one; it's blue! ACTORS 1 and 2 are aghast. A blue nose? That's different. That's just wrong! They convey their abhorrence to the audience. Then ACTOR 1 signals ACTOR 2 with a honk of his/her nose. ACTOR 2 responds with a similar honk back to ACTOR 1. They both look at ACTOR 3, who looks back at both and gives his/her round nose a squeeze. This produces a totally different sound from the others. *(Anything from an electronic buzzer to a duck's quack will do. Just something completely different.)* ACTORS 1 and 2 now recoil in horror and repugnance, their noses utterly out of joint.

Again they exchange glances and then silently begin to goad each other to taunt ACTOR 3 about his/her difference, to rub his/her nose in it, so to speak. After a while, ACTOR 1 slowly approaches 3 and gives his/her blue beak an angry little poke. It makes its strange sound! ACTOR 1 backs off and ACTOR 2 follows suit, also poking the blue nose, which sounds off again. They continue thusly with increasing speed and vehemence, and with each poke or squeeze that blue nose generates its noise. Finally, having gotten completely carried away with their harassment, the two simultaneously give a hard slap to ACTOR 3's nose! There is a loud sound of shattering glass.

Everything stops. The actors freeze. Hesitantly, after a long nervous moment, ACTOR 3 tests his/her nose with a little poke or squeeze. Nothing. No sound. Another test. Still no sound. The other two give it a try. Dead silence. Clearly ACTOR 3's nose is broken. ACTORS 1 and 2 may briefly appear a bit sheepish, but not too terribly so. They both sneak a honk of their own noses just to make sure they're still working. They are. Whew. No skin off their noses. Now they can start to enjoy their cruel accomplishment— congratulating each other, pointing derisively at ACTOR 3, thumbing their noses at him/her, etc.

ACTOR 3, of course, is initially stunned and shaken by this maltreatment. But he/she refuses to let this get him/her down. He/she knows that being different is special. And he/she is going to show that to the others. ACTOR 3 removes the blue nose—evoking a gasp from the others— and then begins to bounce it on the floor! *(This easy trick is accomplished by ACTOR 3 simply palming the nose and trading it for a real blue ball of the same size, such as one used in squash or racquetball.)*

Their initial shock over and despite themselves, ACTORS 1 and 2 begin to grow intrigued by this remarkable blue schnoz. This is something they've never seen before. Soon, music begins, picking up in tempo as it proceeds. The song is something in the spirit of the Harlem Globetrotters' theme "Sweet Georgia Brown," if not that very tune itself. Before long, ACTOR 3 is enjoying all sorts of solo ball-bouncing tricks, e.g., one-ball reverse cascades, under-the-leg bounces, kick-backs, the application of forward and/or backward spin, etc. *(Examples of these can be found on the website www.jugglingworld.biz and other sites, but the performer should feel free to improvise. What's most important is simply to be playful.)* ACTOR 3 might even bounce that nose to—or off of—ACTORS 1 and 2, whose curiosity turns to a bewildered astonishment. Eventually, the music and bouncing both draw to a close. ACTOR 3 puts his/her nose back on and exits triumphantly, perhaps now whistling the bouncy tune.

ACTORS 1 and 2 look at each other. How could this have happened right under their noses? They each excitedly remove their own noses and toss them to the ground. But instead of bouncing, their red snouts take a nosedive, landing with a loud, comical thud. *(This trick is accomplished much as the other, with the actors palming their noses and tossing down a nose-sized ball of red modeling clay.)* The two formerly hard-nosed actors look at each other in horror and rush to retrieve their noses but in their haste accidentally step on those noses, which are squashed flat, producing some horribly sad sound. Peeling the pancake-like noses off of the floor—or the bottom of their shoes, ACTORS 1 and 2 hold them up, look at those ruined noses, at each other, and then out to the audience with a depth of despair quite as plain as the nose on your face.

END OF PLAY

"Send"

By Linda Daugherty

CHARACTERS

ALYSSA	a teenager
JOSHUA	a teenager
SARA	a teenager
NATALIE	a teenager
MIA	a teenager
J.D.	a teenager
KEVIN	a teenager

SETTING AND TIME: Bare stage with props. The present.

(ALYSSA and JOSHUA enter from opposite directions. They stand side by side center and speak to the audience. BOTH hold a cell phone.)

ALYSSA. I'm Alyssa.

JOSHUA. I'm Joshua.

ALYSSA. It started in history.

JOSHUA. We got assigned to do the project together.

ALYSSA. I thought he was hot.

JOSHUA. I thought she was hot.

ALYSSA. We had fun doing the project.

JOSHUA. I really liked her.

ALYSSA. I really liked him. He started texting me.

JOSHUA. She was my girlfriend. So I sent her a picture. I don't remember if she asked me first or I asked her.

211

ALYSSA. Hey, why don't you send me a picture?

JOSHUA. So I did.

ALYSSA. So he did.

JOSHUA. Everybody's doing it, sending pictures.

ALYSSA. In the picture he didn't have his shirt on.

JOSHUA. Guys at school were always sending pictures like that. We were just flirting. Kinda high-tech flirting, I guess.

ALYSSA. And then—

JOSHUA. And then—

ALYSSA. And then…he asked for a picture of *me*.

JOSHUA. Hey, send me a picture.

ALYSSA. It was Saturday morning. I was in my bathroom. My phone was by the sink. I had this feeling that maybe, maybe—I guess I didn't think. I was standing in front of the bathroom mirror after my shower. So I didn't have any clothes on. *(With difficulty.)* I was, I was naked. I took the picture. And I pushed "send." *(She stares out a moment, remembering.)*

ALYSSA & JOSHUA. We broke up a couple of weeks later.

(ALYSSA turns her back to the audience. SARA enters. ALYSSA is between JOSHUA and SARA who look at each other, flirting.)

JOSHUA. So…you like me?

SARA. Yeah.

JOSHUA. A lot?

SARA. Maybe. So you used to be with Alyssa?

JOSHUA. Yeah.

SARA. You still like her?

JOSHUA. Not anymore.

SARA. You sure?

JOSHUA. Yeah. I'm sure.

SARA. We usta be sorta good friends. But I don't hang out with Alyssa anymore. She's so annoying.

JOSHUA. Hey, send me a picture.

SARA. You first.

JOSHUA. Okay.

SARA. Hey...did Alyssa send you any pictures?

JOSHUA. I guess.

SARA. Did she?

JOSHUA. Well, yeah...*one.*

SARA. Send it to me.

JOSHUA. No.

SARA *(begging, flirting).* Come on. Pleeeease.

JOSHUA. Naw.

SARA. You like me?

JOSHUA. Yeah.

SARA. Prove it. Send me that picture of Alyssa.

(JOSHUA and SARA smile at each other, then speak to the audience.)

JOSHUA. So I did.

SARA. So he did. *(Looking at cell phone, shocked.)* She's naked! I mean *totally*! *(She sneers at cell phone.)* Alyssa's trash. I always knew it.

(They continue addressing the audience.)

JOSHUA. So...you got her picture?

SARA. Oh, yeah.

JOSHUA. You deleted it, right?

SARA. Oh, yeah. Sure...

JOSHUA. I guess...I *knew* I shouldn't have sent that picture to Sara. But I did.

SARA. I guess...I *knew* I should have deleted it. But I was sick of Alyssa. So I sent it on. *(Texting on cell phone.)* "Trash alert! If you think Alyssa is trash, send this picture to all your friends!" *(Smiling and holding up cell phone.)* My phone's got a *long* list of contacts.

(ALYSSA turns to audience. NATALIE and MIA enter R and J.D. and KEVIN enter L. ALL have cell phones and speak to the audience.)

ALYSSA. Twenty-four hours later.
JOSHUA & SARA. Twenty-four hours later.
NATALIE, MIA, J.D. & KEVIN. Twenty-four hours later.

(SARA rushes to NATALIE and MIA R. They snicker and whisper together, looking at their cell phones. J.D. and KEVIN, apart L, furtively look at KEVIN's cell phone. JOSHUA texts. ALYSSA tentatively approaches the group of GIRLS.)

ALYSSA. Hey...
NATALIE. Oh, uh, hi, Alyssa.
ALYSSA. You guys going to lunch?
NATALIE. Uh, no. I'm not really hungry.
MIA. Yeah, me either.
SARA *(reacts excitedly as if receiving text)*. Sorry, I'm meeting... *(pointedly to ALYSSA)* ...someone.

(SARA rushes to JOSHUA. They greet each other and turn, both with backs to the audience.)

MIA. I, uh, gotta go.
NATALIE. Uh, yeah, me too.

MIA *(intimately to NATALIE but for ALYSSA's benefit).* Hey, listen, we gotta send some people that picture!

(MIA and NATALIE exit R, laughing and gossiping. ALYSSA watches them go.)

J.D. *(snatching cell phone from KEVIN, calls to ALYSSA and waves phone in the air, pointing at screen).* Hey, Alyssa! Amazing!

KEVIN *(embarrassed and trying to grab cell phone from J.D.).* Shut up, J.D.! Give me my phone!

J.D. Take some pictures for *me*, Alyssa!

KEVIN. Come on, man!

J.D. You know, like you did for Joshua!

KEVIN *(grabbing phone from J.D. and pulling him off).* Give me my phone, moron!

(KEVIN and J.D. exit.)

ALYSSA *(to audience).* It was like I was walking down the hallways of my school…naked. I ate lunch alone. Every day. Nobody called. Nobody texted me. I didn't want to come out of my room. I made a plan to change schools after winter break. My mom didn't know why I was unhappy. But she said okay. I knew a few kids at the new school. I was feeling happy about the change. But the night before—

(NATALIE and MIA enter R. J.D. and KEVIN enter L. ALL are looking at their cell phones.)

ALYSSA. The night before—in the middle of the night—

(NATALIE, MIA, J.D. and KEVIN begin rapidly texting and snickering.)

ALYSSA. My phone—it woke me up.
NATALIE *(pushing button on cell phone)*. Send!
MIA *(pushing button on cell phone)*. Send!
J.D. *(pushing button on cell phone)*. Send!
KEVIN *(pushing button on cell phone)*. Send!

(NATALIE, MIA, J.D. and KEVIN continue rapidly texting and laughing.)

ALYSSA. One friend sent it to another. And another. And another! All night long! They sent my picture to kids at the new school! Nearly everyone!
NATALIE, MIA, J.D. & KEVIN *(simultaneously pushing buttons on cell phones)*. Send!!! *(They turn backs to audience.)*
ALYSSA. I didn't change schools. Didn't go anywhere. Didn't talk to anyone. That week someone's mom saw the picture on her kid's phone and called my mom. She sent her the picture. My mom went nuts. She phoned the principal. The principal called a meeting. And the principal called the cops.

(ALYSSA turns her back to the audience. JOSHUA and SARA turn and speak to the audience.)

JOSHUA. They came to my house.
SARA. They came to my house.
JOSHUA. I mean, everybody does it.
SARA. Everybody sends those pictures.
JOSHUA. It makes you look cool.
SARA. It makes you look sexy.

JOSHUA. Adults do it.

SARA. You see it on TV. That Super Bowl commercial? Remember? This model's in a bubble bath and she snaps a picture for her boyfriend.

JOSHUA. In songs the guy asks the girl to send him a dirty picture. Snap.

SARA. You see it in the movies.

JOSHUA. Hey, a famous football player did it.

SARA. Even a big congressman in Washington did it.

(JOSHUA and SARA each cross one hand over the other as if handcuffed.)

JOSHUA. They came to my house.

SARA. They came to my house.

JOSHUA. I didn't know it was against the law.

SARA. I didn't know it was against the law.

JOSHUA. They put me in handcuffs.

SARA. They put me in handcuffs.

JOSHUA & SARA. They took me to juvie.

SARA. I had to stay overnight.

JOSHUA. They took my clothes.

JOSHUA & SARA. Could it be on my record forever?

ALYSSA *(turns to the audience)*. I heard about the arrests. I thought they'd come for me, too. But they didn't. At the meeting, the prosecutor said I'd already learned my lesson…a thousand times over.

(NATALIE, MIA, J.D. and KEVIN turn to audience. ALL speak to the audience.)

JOSHUA. I'm, I'm ashamed of what I did.

SARA. I asked Alyssa to forgive me. She didn't say anything. Just stared at me.

ALYSSA. Some days—most days…I just can't get out of
  bed.
  (After a moment…)

NATALIE. I didn't think…
J.D. *(overlapping NATALIE)*. I didn't think...
MIA & KEVIN *(overlapping J.D.)*. I didn't think...
JOSHUA & SARA. *(overlapping MIA and KEVIN)*. I didn't
  think.
ALYSSA. Once it's done.
JOSHUA. Once you've pushed "send"…
SARA. Once you've pushed "send"…
NATALIE & J.D. Once you've pushed "send"…
MIA & KEVIN. Once you've pushed "send"…
ALYSSA. You can't take it back.
ALL. You can never take it back.
ALYSSA. Never.
ALL. Once you've pushed "send."

END OF PLAY

The Shirt

By R.N. Sandberg

CHARACTERS

HARDY .... a teenager, male or female
BEAMS .... a teenager, male or female
FLOW .... a teenager, male or female
SILK .... a teenager, male or female

NOTE: Be aware that different dynamics will be created by various gender casting.

SETTING AND TIME: Bare stage with props. The present.

(BEAMS wears an unbuttoned shirt over a top. HARDY enters.)

HARDY. Hey.
BEAMS. Oh no.
HARDY. That is the ugliest shirt I've ever seen.
BEAMS. Here we go again.
HARDY. You find it in the trash?
BEAMS. My mother gave it to me, actually.
HARDY. What, is she blind? Color blind, anyway!
BEAMS. Ha. Ha.
HARDY. Where ya goin'? Runnin' home to mommy? Oh poor baby. Please buy me another pretty shirt, mommy. Please, please, please.
BEAMS. You know, you're an idiot.

HARDY. And you're a stupid freak.

BEAMS. Ooh, that hurts. Especially coming from you. I've always looked up to you as someone with great intelligence and sensitivity. *(HARDY grabs BEAMS.)* Ow. Lemme go.

HARDY. Why? You don't like me?

BEAMS. Yeah, like I like tsunamis. Ow.

HARDY. Maybe I oughta tsunami you.

BEAMS. Stop.

HARDY. Make your mascara run. Mess up your pretty face.

BEAMS. You're gonna rip the shirt.

HARDY. Oh, your beautiful shirt.

BEAMS. C'mon, it's gonna tear.

HARDY. What? You afraid mama'll be mad? Afraid some-one'll get to see your beautiful body?

BEAMS. Yeah, someone like you. Someone fixated on bodies.

HARDY *(pushes BEAMS away)*. Take it off.

BEAMS. What is wrong with you?

HARDY. Take off the stupid shirt.

BEAMS. No.

HARDY. What?

BEAMS. I won't.

HARDY. You take it off or I'll rip it off you.

BEAMS. Fine. It's yours. *(Throws the shirt at HARDY.)* It'll probably look even more beautiful on you.

HARDY. I'm—I'm gonna burn it.

BEAMS. Watch out you don't set yourself on fire. Matches are dangerous for kids, you know.

HARDY. Get down. Down on the ground.

BEAMS. Okay. What are we gonna do now?

HARDY. Take off—take off your shoes.

BEAMS. I don't think they'll fit you. And I believe they'll be rather difficult to burn.

HARDY. Take 'em off.

BEAMS. Don't you ever get tired of this? I mean, my shirt, my shoes, my coat, my bag. I'd think you'd get bored. There. Now what?

HARDY. Now, get out of here. I've had enough of you.

BEAMS. You sure? You don't want me to—I don't know? Take something else off? My jeans maybe?

HARDY. Get out before you really get hurt.

BEAMS. I don't mind taking them off. I don't think they'd fit you but they'd probably burn okay.

HARDY. You want me to hurt you?

BEAMS. Why is it you like to grab me so much? You're always pulling me close, pressing up against me, whispering some obscenity in my ear. And now, get on the ground. Take it off. Take it off. Wow.

HARDY. What are you sayin'? You sayin' I'm gay? You're the one who's gay. You're so gay it stinks off you.

BEAMS. Is that why you keep coming after me? You need to be all up against my gayness? Need it to rub all over you?

HARDY. You wish.

BEAMS. No, I don't actually. I'm perfectly happy to keep my gayness all for myself. I really don't need to share it with anyone. If you need some, I'd actually prefer you find it from someone who isn't happy with it, who wants to get rid of it, who'd be thrilled to be your plaything. But really, that's not me. As exciting as our meetings are, they really aren't a turn-on. Are they for you? I mean, really. Late at night, when you're all alone, do you think about these—encounters? Do they make you feel all warm inside? Like you can't wait for the next one? Somehow, I'm guessing they aren't really all that satisfying. Me? I'd rather read a book, go shopping for diamond studs, dance. So if it's okay with you, can we just put an end to these little secret meetings?

HARDY. Take your stupid shirt.

BEAMS. You know what? The shoes, yes. But that shirt? You really seemed to want it. So it's a gift. From me to you.

(BEAMS exits. HARDY throws the shirt down. Is troubled. Then picks it up. Looks at it. Laughs. Puts on the shirt. But is still troubled.

FLOW backs onto the stage, looking off, still upset by something that's happened.)

FLOW. Stupid? You're the one who's stupid. *(Sees HARDY and smiles.)* Hey? Hardy? Whoa, nice shirt.

HARDY. Shut up.

FLOW. Nah, really. Looks good.

HARDY. Right.

FLOW. It's hot!

HARDY. You think I look hot?

FLOW. Sharp! Anybody see you in that, oo-wee, they gonna go crazy.

HARDY. You're crazy.

FLOW. All right, don't believe me.

HARDY. I never believe you.

FLOW. That's your problem, then, isn't it?

HARDY. You really think it looks good?

FLOW. Do I lie?

HARDY. Yeah, Flow. You lie all the time.

FLOW. Nah, you think I do, 'cause you don't really listen. You don't listen to nobody. You too busy listenin' to yerself. But I'm truth tellin' twenty-four seven.

HARDY. Yeah?

FLOW. You wanna know something else?

HARDY. Now that we're truth tellin'.

FLOW. You got a self-esteem problem.

HARDY. Gimme a break.

FLOW. Nah. Nobody can't tell you nothin'. You know everythin'. You the best at everythin'. Ev'rybody just shut up when you around 'cause you gotta spew yer spit. Lift yerself like t' the treetops, to some cloud, 'cause otherwise you be drownin'. It's sad. You sad. Now, what? You gonna bust me one?

HARDY. You really think that? That's the way I am? Sad? Do you really think that, Flow?

FLOW. I don't know. Nah. I'm just—I'm just—it's me. Been screwin' up all over today. I don't know what I'm talkin' about.

HARDY. So—the shirt really didn't look good.

FLOW. Nah, the shirt's cool.

HARDY. You—you want it?

FLOW. Nah, it looks real good on you.

HARDY. I think it's ugly.

FLOW. Nah, it's good material. Feel it. Expensive. You can see that a mile away. I mean it musta cost, what? A lot, right?

HARDY. Yeah, a lot.

FLOW. You walk through the halls with that, they be swoonin'. Thinkin' c'ching, c'ching, c'ching.

HARDY. You take it.

FLOW. You sure?

HARDY. Doesn't feel right.

FLOW. Well, ya don't got to say it twice. You know it's gonnna look nice here. Hand it over. This is my color, too. Right? You know that! Tell me it's not my color!

HARDY. It looks good. You look good.

FLOW. Hey? Sorry for what I said before. That was all about me.

HARDY. Yeah, sure. *(Thinking.)*

FLOW. But whoa, I love this shirt! I love this shirt! Wearin' this shirt makes life perfect! Nobody can stop me now!

(SILK enters. FLOW stops and stares at SILK. SILK is looking at HARDY who's still deep in thought.)

FLOW. Hey.

SILK *(to HARDY)*. What's wrong with you?

HARDY. Nothin'.

FLOW. Hey, Silk.

SILK *(to HARDY)*. Somebody just die?

HARDY. I said nothing.

FLOW. Hey, Silk, look here.

SILK *(to HARDY)*. You got that much love for me, you're gonna send me runnin'.

FLOW. This is hot, right? This is sharp!

SILK. Look, I told you before, we're finished. I got nothing to do with you.

FLOW. Yeah, but that was before, right? Now, I got this. My color. Tight fit. Material that makes you wanna cry, right? Sharp.

SILK. Yeah, I'm crying all right.

FLOW. Hey, you wanna know why Hardy's lookin' all beat? 'Cause I got the shirt! Buyer's regret, or whatever they call it. Had it on before but gave it to me. Now, sorry I'm the one sportin'. Told you you shoulda kept it. Then you'd be happy to see Silk. Now it's me who's sharp.

HARDY. I gotta go.

SILK. I just got here.

FLOW. Who cares? Let Hardy go. I'm lookin' good. You're lookin' good. We gonna have a good time now, right?

SILK. Yeah, you're right. What was I thinking? Hardy, you can go. I just wanna be with Flow here. I mean, look at that shirt. The color? The tight fit? That is sharp. Isn't that sharp? You're sharp with that shirt, Flow. You're sharp every which way. You know what? When I think of sharp, I think of you. You're the walking definition of sharp. Sharp clothes, sharp mind, sharp personality. When I've got a homework problem I just can't penetrate, who'm I gonna go to? Gotta be you. You're sharp. You'll just get right to it. When I got a personal problem, when I really need to work out a relationship? You know where I'm gonna turn. 'Cause you'll let me know just how I need to stick to that person, how to stick it to 'im, right? Sharp. I'm amazed I never realized. Guess that must be why I begged you never to leave my side ever again. Why you're the most important person in my life. You're special. So special. Not like any other person in the world.

FLOW. Yeah, okay. I got it.

SILK. That makes me very happy. It must make you very happy, too. C'mon, Hardy, let's get out of here. Hardy?

HARDY. Hey? Flow? The shirt looks good.

FLOW. Right.

HARDY. It looks good on you. You look good in that shirt. You look good.

SILK. You have lost your mind. Your eyesight and your mind.

HARDY. Could be.

FLOW. I told you. This is a bad, bad day.

SILK. For you. 'Cause every day's a bad day for you.

HARDY. Let it be, okay?

SILK. You're gonna tell me to let it be?

HARDY. I'm asking, OK? You want people to not be idiots, you gotta, I don't know, stand back. Let 'em breathe a little.

SILK. Ooo, we're getting heavy now.

HARDY. Yeah. I'm an idiot, too. You're right.

SILK. I am finding myself in unknown territory here.

HARDY. Lost one whole half my mind.

SILK. So how much does that leave you with?

FLOW. Half, right?

SILK *(laughs)*. Is there hope for you? Is there any hope for you, Flow? Tell me.

HARDY. There's hope. There's always hope.

SILK. Unknown territory.

HARDY. Hey look, the shirt is good all right. Flow's good and so is the shirt.

SILK. What is with this stupid shirt?

FLOW. It's good. It's sharp.

HARDY. It is. But, Flow? I want it back. I know I gave it to you. And I know you like it. I know you love it.

FLOW. And you know it looks good.

HARDY. And I know it looks good. But I need it back.

FLOW. Your shirt. Your call. But when I see you wearin' it and ev'rybody's goin' like c'ching, c'ching, you be pointing my way sayin' there's the generosity that's making you look so good.

SILK. I am about to throw up inside my mouth.

FLOW. Just don't get it on yer shirt. You lookin' bad enough without that! Ha!

HARDY. I'd say that, Flow, but I won't be wearing it. It's— it's a gift for someone. *(Exits with the shirt.)*

FLOW. So, you wanna hang out?

(SILK stares after HARDY.)

END OF PLAY

We're Your Friends

By Werner Trieschmann

CHARACTERS

CINDY .... a high-school student
STACY .... a high-school student
AMY .... a high-school student

SETTING AND TIME: Locations in and around high school. Three stools—the two on the ends are slightly taller than the one in the middle—in front of a screen or wall. The present.

Scene 1: The Bathroom

(A school BELL or BUZZER goes off.

CINDY walks out from behind the screen and stands in front of the middle stool. She looks straight ahead as if standing in front of a mirror.

A moment where CINDY takes in her appearance and reacts in a way that is not joyous but certainly content.

AMY and STACY now walk out at the same time and stand beside CINDY. They are dressed in a decidedly more glamorous/racy manner than CINDY. AMY and STACY glance at CINDY and then shoot a look at each

other. AMY and STACY now check themselves out in the
mirror.)

AMY *(to CINDY)*. We're your friends.

STACY. Yeah, we're your friends, Cindy.

CINDY. I know.

AMY. So?

STACY. Seriously.

AMY. I mean, Cindy—

CINDY. What?

STACY. You did like *look* at yourself before—

AMY. —before, you know, you *left*.

STACY. Seriously.

CINDY. What is it? What's wrong?

AMY *(to STACY)*. Did she just really ask that?

STACY *(to AMY)*. She really did.

CINDY. Stacy?

AMY *(looking at herself in the mirror)*. Oh my God, this
    lipstick is like the best! I look so incredible in this
    lipstick!

CINDY. Amy?

STACY. We're your friends.

AMY *(to CINDY)*. You only wish you looked this incredibly
    hot in this lipstick. You only wish!

CINDY. Could I try it?

AMY *(almost shrieking)*. Do you know how much this
    cost?!

AMY *(to STACY about CINDY)*. Anyway, lipstick wouldn't
    help your cause.

STACY. Remember. We're your friends.

AMY. Yeah.

CINDY. I know. Would you tell me what's wrong?

AMY. For one thing, those clothes—

STACY. Seriously.

AMY. Is that like your mom's outfit or something?

STACY. Do you think Jeremy is going to notice you like that?

AMY *(to STACY)*. Oh little Jeremy, band nerd Jeremy?

CINDY. He said hi to me after first period.

AMY. Yeah, well, it's probably the last time, as those clothes are hideous.

STACY. Hideous.

AMY. We're your friends, Cindy.

STACY. Seriously. Hideous.

(The BELL or BUZZER goes off.

AMY and STACY look in the mirror one last time and then turn and walk behind the screen. CINDY looks in the mirror with a frown and then walks out.

LIGHTS down.)

Scene 2: The Movie Theatre

(LIGHTS up as AMY and STACY, wearing 3D glasses and holding boxes of popcorn, walk out and sit on their stools.)

AMY. That vampire is so hot!

STACY. I like the werewolf.

AMY. So is she coming with the stuff or not?

STACY. Seriously. She better. I like need it 'cause these glasses are givin' me a headache.

AMY. You are so wrong. That vampire is so hot!

(CINDY, now wearing clothes like AMY's and STACY's from the first scene, as well as 3D glasses, walks in. She is carrying a big purse.)

AMY *(to CINDY)*. Like, hello, the movie started twenty minutes ago.

STACY *(to CINDY)*. Yeah, like, hello!

CINDY. Sorry. I almost… I was nervous.

STACY *(grabbing the purse)*. We're your friends.

AMY. Yeah.

CINDY. Is there a manager…?

AMY. Oh my God, a manager? I think there's somebody having sex back there. Who cares?

(STACY now has the bottle of whiskey out of CINDY's purse and is taking a drink.)

AMY *(cont'd)*. Gimmie! *(She reaches over and grabs the bottle from STACY.)*

STACY *(to CINDY)*. So are you vampire or werewolf?

(AMY hands the bottle to CINDY. CINDY takes it but is clearly nervous.)

AMY *(to STACY)*. She's a vampire!

STACY *(to AMY)*. She's a werewolf!

AMY *(to STACY)*. A vampire!

STACY *(to AMY)*. Werewolf!

AMY *(to CINDY)*. So?!

STACY. Oh, I know! She's a chicken!

AMY. Ha! Good one!

(AMY notices CINDY is just holding the bottle.)

AMY *(cont'd. To CINDY)*. You gonna drink or what?

CINDY. Doesn't it burn your throat?

AMY. If you don't take a drink, I'll stand up and yell that you brought it in.

STACY *(to AMY)*. Oh you should so do that anyway!

CINDY. No! Please!

(CINDY takes a small drink and reacts. STACY grabs the bottle from her.)

AMY *(to CINDY)*. You know, I think I saw your little Jeremy back there.

CINDY. What?

STACY. Yeah. He was with somebody.

AMY. No, it was like he was on top of somebody. That was the couple that was going at it.

CINDY. Really?

AMY. God, Cindy, even I thought you had a shot at a band nerd.

STACY. Guess not.

AMY. Guess not.

STACY. We're your friends.

AMY. Yeah. We know. Maybe you should set your sights lower.

STACY. What's the name of that kid that drools and has the big head?

AMY *(to STACY)*. Good one!

(CINDY grabs the bottle and slugs it back. STACY and AMY lift up their glasses and look as CINDY drinks.

LIGHTS down.)

Scene 3: In the Car

(LIGHTS up on AMY, who is driving, with CINDY in the middle and STACY by the window.)

AMY. God, I hate this dead town and the stupid dead people in it.

STACY. For sure.

AMY *(out the window)*. YOU PEOPLE ALL…SUCK!

STACY. Can't wait until I put this place in my rearview mirror. See ya! You'll all see me when I'm a…

AMY. Model.

STACY. Or a doctor.

AMY *(looking out the window)*. Here's this town. Crappy fast-food restaurant. Gas station. Starbucks. Crappy fast-food restaurant. Repeat.

STACY. This town is more your speed, Cindy.

CINDY. I know. I am going to stay here.

STACY. Tell us something we don't know.

CINDY. I mean, I'm going to the university.

AMY. Yeah, you'll fit in there.

CINDY. I think I am going to be a veterinarian.

AMY. A what?

CINDY. Take care of animals.

AMY. You gotta be smart to do that, right? Like we said, aim lower. Start by cleaning up their poop.

STACY. Ha! Good one!

AMY *(to CINDY)*. Yeah. Stay here. Have babies here.

CINDY. You'll come back for summers, right? Are you coming back, Stacy? Amy?

STACY. Maybe to get money from my parents.

AMY *(to CINDY)*. You think we'll come back and pick you up and it'll be like high school all over again?

CINDY. It could be that way, couldn't it?

STACY. Seriously?

AMY. No. We're gone. And too bad for you. You won't ever have friends like us.

STACY. You won't know how to dress.

AMY. How to have fun.

STACY. Or anything about boys.

AMY. You're clueless about boys.

CINDY. I know.

AMY. You won't ever have friends like us.

STACY. Seriously.

CINDY *(hopefully, with a slight smile)*. I know. I know.

(LIGHTS down.)

END OF PLAY

What Goes Around

By D.W. Gregory

CHARACTERS

BOSS (EVERETT BLEDSOE)................a sales director for a beauty products supply company
SMEDLEY ....an ineffective salesman for the same company
JUNIOR...Smedley's son, 12
DARLA ....Smedley's daughter, 14
MARCIE .... a girl on the school bus
GANG ....as much a mentality as a group, to be performed by one to three or more actors
MRS. NICKLES.................................a school administrator
ANNOUNCER
DRIVER

NOTE: The play is expandable and playable with a single table, which doubles as a desk, dining table, bus, etc., and several chairs. The Gang's lines may be divided among the actors assigned to the role according to the needs of the production. The play could also be performed by four adult actors, doubling as follows:

BOSS/ANNOUNCER/MARCIE   JUNIOR/DRIVER
SMEDLEY/GANG   DARLA/NICKLES

These would be two different experiences, no doubt, but the point should be the same.

SETTING AND TIME: Bare stage with props. The present.

(An office, represented by a table that stands in for a desk, and two chairs. Behind the table stands the BOSS, with a folder. SMEDLEY sits in a chair opposite, sinking further and further into his own misery.)

BOSS. Results, Smedley.

SMEDLEY. Uh—

BOSS. Results!

SMEDLEY. I—

BOSS. Down fifteen percent over the fourth quarter— fifteen percent—what do you call that, Smedley?

SMEDLEY. The economy—

BOSS *(cutting him off)*. Disaster. That's what you call it. When your numbers fall off a cliff!

SMEDLEY. It's not that bad really, considering—

BOSS *(cutting him off, not letting him get in a word)*. Smedley! Put a couple brain cells together, if you can. Your numbers are going down. That's not the right direction, is it? Because we want them to go UP! Now, why do you suppose that is, Smedley? Do you have a clue? I'll tell you! Because we're in business to make money, you see, and when sales go down—WE DON'T MAKE MONEY!

(A beat. SMEDLEY clears his throat.)

SMEDLEY *(a deep breath)*. Mr. Bledsoe. I really think the situation in Seattle—

BOSS. Seattle? That's your explanation? A tiny little earth-quake on the West Coast—and you can't make your sales quota?

SMEDLEY. It was seven-point-six on the Richter scale.

BOSS. Yesterday's news!

SMEDLEY. Half of our West Coast business is in Seattle.

BOSS. What's your point?

SMEDLEY. There's just not much demand for nail polish after an earthquake.

BOSS *(after a beat)*. I would think if a woman's house had been leveled flat—she'd take some comfort in being well-groomed.

SMEDLEY *(eagerly)*. Well, you would think! *(More somber.)* Except—the nail parlors have been leveled along with the houses. So when you think about it, a fifteen percent drop is actually—holding our own. It's actually—surprisingly good. Considering...

(A longer beat. The BOSS thinks about this argument. Then, calmly...)

BOSS. Smedley. What you're giving me...is not an explanation.

SMEDLEY. But—

BOSS. It's an excuse. And you know who makes excuses? Losers.

SMEDLEY. But the—

BOSS. Losers make excuses, Smedley. Losers. The guys in the back row. The ones who trip over their own shoelaces. Who can't even tie their shoes! They're back there, on the ground, whining—while the first guy is already over the finish line. Because he is not blaming an earthquake for his poor performance!

SMEDLEY. I— *(A beat.)* Okay. I see your point...

BOSS. And Smedley? I don't work with losers.

SMEDLEY *(after a beat)*. Are you saying? What is it you're saying, exactly, Mr. Bledsoe?

BOSS. I. Don't. Work. With. Losers.

SMEDLEY *(with sinking hopes)*. So this isn't a friendly warning then? *(BOSS points violently towards the exit.*

SMEDLEY looks in the direction of where he is pointing.)
Oh boy.

(LIGHT shift. BOSS and SMEDLEY shift the table and arrange the chairs in front of it to create some bleachers in a ballpark. BOSS leaves, SMEDLEY sits on the table and DARLA enters and joins him. She has a cell phone and is busy texting. LIGHT bump and SMEDLEY watches anxiously as his son, JUNIOR, offstage, is up to bat in a ballgame that is going badly for his team.)

SMEDLEY. Settle in. Come on. You'll never get a hit like that. Quit bouncing around!

(Beat. Offstage, JUNIOR swings and misses. SOUND effect: crowd reaction.)

SMEDLEY *(in pain)*. Oh! *(DARLA continues to text.)* All you have to do is hit the ball. *(A beat.)* How hard is it to hit the ball?

(DARLA continues to text. Offstage, JUNIOR swings and misses. Crowd effect: BOOS and CHEERS. SMEDLEY is disgusted.)

SMEDLEY *(cont'd)*. Come on. The bases are loaded— you're gonna blow it for everybody.

(He watches anxiously. Offstage, JUNIOR swings and misses. Crowd effect.)

ANNOUNCER. And that's the ball game! Midville Majors take it 7-O *(pronounced seven-oh)*.
SMEDLEY. Ah, for cryin' out loud!

(DARLA takes no notice. Enter JUNIOR.)

SMEDLEY *(cont'd. Sourly).* Good going out there. What do you call that? Some kind of a barn dance?

(DARLA snickers.)

JUNIOR. Barn dance?

SMEDLEY. The way you were moving around. No wonder you couldn't get a hit.

JUNIOR. The sun was in my eyes.

SMEDLEY. Only losers make excuses.

JUNIOR. What do you want me to do?

SMEDLEY. Hit the ball, turkey!

JUNIOR. I just want to go home.

SMEDLEY. Let me explain something to you, son. This world is divided into two kinds of people. Winners and *losers*. You know who the losers are?

JUNIOR. Other kids?

SMEDLEY. Kids with bad attitudes. Kids who don't practice, who don't focus. Who whine and complain. They're back there, on the ground, still trying to tie their shoes, while the rest of the team is over the finish line!

DARLA. There's no finish line in baseball.

SMEDLEY. It's a metaphor.

JUNIOR *(under his breath).* I hate baseball.

SMEDLEY. Nobody hates baseball! What's the matter with you? *(He yanks JUNIOR's cap off his head. To DARLA.)* What are you laughing at?

DARLA. Nothing.

SMEDLEY. The two of you—have got the worst attitudes of any kids I ever saw.

DARLA. What did I do?

SMEDLEY. You take up space.

(Now JUNIOR snickers. SMEDLEY grabs DARLA's phone.)

DARLA. Dad!
SMEDLEY. I saw your report card this morning. You're not getting this back till you get your grades up.

(SMEDLEY pockets the phone and leaves. A beat. DARLA sees JUNIOR looking at her.)

DARLA *(threatening)*. What are you looking at?
JUNIOR. Nothing.

(FREEZE, then a LIGHT shift. Enter the GANG and the DRIVER. They bring in chairs and arrange the scene to create the sense of a school bus. The GANG, JUNIOR and DARLA sit. JUNIOR reads a comic book. DARLA complains to the GANG.)

DARLA. So I'm like so not listening to him, but he's like insane! I'm like, "Dad! How am I going to talk to my friends if you take my phone?" And he's like, "You got a C-minus in geometry!" Like, anybody really needs to know geometry. I mean, come on, who even *goes* to geometry class?

(During this, MARCIE has entered and approaches to wait for the bus. MARCIE is awkward, dressed rather oddly, compared to the group. She carries several books.)

GANG #1. You mean, besides her?

(DRIVER makes SOUND of the bus screeching to a halt.)

DARLA. What is she doing on the bus? She never rides the bus.

GANG #1. Guess her dad got sick of driving her.

GANG #2. You ever notice how she doesn't look at people? When she talks to them?

GANG #3. It's like she just looks at their shoes.

DARLA. She must have a thing for shoes.

GANG #3. Or feet.

DARLA. Ooh, don't take me there! Please. That's just too— eh.

GANG #1. No way am I sitting next to that.

DARLA. It would definitely knock us back, socially speaking, to be seen sitting with that.

(MARCIE gets on the bus and tries to find a seat. The GANG moves to make sure she cannot find a seat.)

MARCIE. Excuse me.
DARLA. Sorry. It's saved.

(MARCIE moves on.)

GANG #3. Saved.

(MARCIE tries another.)

GANG #2. Saved.

(Not knowing what to do. MARCIE stands at the back of the bus. EVERYONE mimes the motion of a bus on a bumpy road. MARCIE produces a book and reads it as the bus bumps along. JUNIOR, DARLA and GANG confer, quietly. MARCIE sees an opening and sits down.)

GANG #2. I said that's saved.

MARCIE. I'll just sit here till your friend gets on.

GANG #2. Guess again.

(MARCIE turns away and focuses on her book.)

GANG #1 *(to DARLA)*. This thing seems to have a hearing problem.

DARLA. Or a mental problem.

GANG #3. I hear she's a witch.

DARLA. Get real.

GANG #1. She casts spells on people. That's the only way they'll talk to her.

(LAUGHTER all around.)

DARLA. Okay, move it.

MARCIE. Huh?

DARLA. This is our seat—and we don't appreciate it being contaminated with toxic waste.

GANG #2. So get the lead out—

GANG #3. And shove off!

(GANG tries to push MARCIE out of her seat.)

MARCIE. What's your problem?

GANG #3. What's yours?

GANG #1. Is she brain-dead or what?

DARLA. Something's not working in there.

(MARCIE tries to get back into the seat.)

GANG #2. This is, what do you call it? Majorly self-destructive behavior.

DARLA. Needs an intervention.

(JUNIOR whispers in DARLA's ear. DARLA whispers in GANG's ear. GANG grabs the book out of MARCIE's hand. MARCIE cries out—GANG tosses the book to DARLA who tosses it to JUNIOR who tosses it to GANG as MARCIE tries to get it back. She turns and sees that GANG #1 has occupied her seat. DRIVER pays no attention to the kids.)

MARCIE. You think you're so smart.
GANG #3. You think you're so smart.
MARCIE. I have a right to a seat.
GANG #1. I have a right to a seat.
DARLA. You don't have a right to my seat.
ALL. And this seat is saved.

(MARCIE moves away. DARLA tosses the book at her.)

DARLA. Don't forget your book. Loser.
GANG #1 *(laughing)*. Good one!

(GANG #1 turns to MARCIE—and sees that she has the book in her hand—they make eye contact—and MARCIE takes a swing at her with the book. A tableau of MARCIE with the book raised and GANG #1 recoiling from the coming blow, and the DRIVER, finally realizing what is going on, turning back to look.)

DRIVER. Hey!

(BLACKOUT. In the black, SOUND of a fight—brief, chaotic, crazy, then...)

DRIVER'S VOICE. You kids knock it off! I don't care how it started!

(Then SILENCE. A voiceover:)

MRS. NICKLES *(voiceover, could be recorded).* We regret to inform you that your daughter has been suspended from the Piedmont School for inappropriate behavior on the bus. This is a serious, serious situation. And requires your immediate attention.

(LIGHTS UP and we see the BOSS sitting in the same sorry position as SMEDLEY in the first scene, sinking into his chair as MRS. NICKLES, the vice principal, stands behind her desk, studying a file. In contrast to the first scene, the BOSS is no longer in the power position, and he knows it.)

MRS. NICKLES. Outside a school context—this little escapade would be considered assault, Mr. Bledsoe.

BOSS. Assault!

MRS. NICKLES. She kicked a boy in the shins.

BOSS. I hardly think—

MRS. NICKLES. Stepped on three sets of toes. Broke one child's iPad. And gave another girl a black eye.

BOSS. My Marcie?

MRS. NICKLES. And when the bus driver tried to intervene—she hit him.

BOSS. Well *that* was an accident.

MRS. NICKLES. Lucky for you, none of the victims' parents plan to press charges.

BOSS. These kids weren't exactly victims here.

MRS. NICKLES. What do you call them?

BOSS. They were picking on her.

MRS. NICKLES. In addition to all that—the bus driver quit. *(Sliding a form across the desk.)* Thirty days' suspension.

BOSS *(looking at the form)*. Thirty days!

MRS. NICKLES. Mr. Bledsoe. We have a zero tolerance policy here at the Piedmont School. Particularly when it comes to fighting on the bus. *(Confidentially.)* Do you have any idea how hard it is to find a qualified bus driver these days? Not easy.

BOSS. I just want you to understand. My Marcie isn't usually like this.

MRS. NICKLES. Indeed?

BOSS. She's had a difficult year. *(Confidentially.)* Her mother and I? We've had some problems...and I think perhaps it's...affected her?

MRS. NICKLES. Mr. Bledsoe. We have a saying here at the Piedmont School: Only losers. Make excuses.

BOSS. Really? Well, that's a pretty good saying...

MRS. NICKLES. And it sounds to me as if you *(with a smile)* are making excuses.

BOSS. I'm not making excuses. I would never make excuses.

MRS. NICKLES. Then I suggest you sign this form.

BOSS. But thirty days...

MRS. NICKLES. The alternative is outright expulsion, Mr. Bledsoe.

BOSS. Expulsion!

MRS. NICKLES. And of course, if your daughter is expelled for fighting on the bus—it would become part of her permanent record.

BOSS. Permanent.

MRS. NICKLES *(quietly threatening)*. Anywhere she goes —it goes with her. With a history of acting out—I doubt any quality school would take her. She might be forced to go to *public* school. *(She says "public" as if it were a disease.)* And need I add, university admission officers would not look kindly at this black mark on her record.

BOSS *(breaking out in a cold sweat)*. There goes Georgetown.

MRS. NICKELS. Exactly. *(She holds out a pen.)*

BOSS *(as he signs, congenially)*. It's a real puzzle to me. The way kids carry on...always having to get the upper hand. You know, be the top dog? Marcie's the same way, to tell you the truth. I don't know where she gets that attitude.

MRS. NICKELS. It's hard to figure. *(She takes the form.)*

END OF PLAY

ABOUT THE PLAYWRIGHTS

Sandra Fenichel Asher's plays have been honored with an NEA grant, three AATE Distinguished Play Awards, the IRT Bonderman Award, NETC's Aurand Harris Award, the Charlotte B. Chorpenning Award for a distinguished body of work, and an Aurand Harris Fellowship grant from the Children's Theatre Foundation of America. Asher is also the author of two dozen books for young readers and the editor of five fiction anthologies.

Visit her at http://usaplays4kids.drury.edu/playwrights/asher

Cherie Bennett is one of the best known writers for family audiences in the country. As a playwright, her many awards include being a two-time winner of New Visions/New Voices at The Kennedy Center. Her play *Anne Frank & Me* ran Off-Broadway to stellar reviews in the *New York Times,* and it continues to be produced all over the world. Cherie has had more than a dozen novels for young adults on the *New York Times* Best Sellers List. In TV, she's won both an Emmy and a Writers Guild Award. She is a popular motivational speaker, and runs writing workshops in middle and high schools. She can be reached about speaking engagements and workshops at: authorchik@aol.com. She lives in Los Angeles with her son, her two cats, her endless belief in young people, and her skewed sense of humor.

Max Bush is a freelance playwright and director whose plays are widely produced on professional, educational and amateur stages across the country. He has won many awards for his work including the AATE Distinguished Play Award IUPUI National Playwriting Competition, and individual artist grants from Michigan Council for the Arts. In 1995, Meriwether Press published an anthology of 10 of his plays, and the AATE awarded him the Charlotte B. Chorpenning Award for a nationally significant body of work for young audiences. In 2003, he was selected by Grand Valley State University to receive the Distinguished Alumni Award.

José Casas' plays have been produced across the country. Works written include *the vine, la rosa still grows beyond the wall* and *14*. His plays *la ofrenda (the offering)* and *somebody's children* have both been awarded the IRT Bonderman Playwriting for Youth Award and the AATE Distinguished Play Award.

Gloria Bond Clunie is a member of the Playwriting Ensemble at the Regional Tony Award-winning Victory Gardens Theater where *North Star, Living Green* and *Shoes* premiered. Other works include *Mercy Rising, DRIP, Sweet Water Taste, Mirandy and Brother Wind, Merry Kwanzaa* and *Quark*. Awards include a Chicago Jeff Award, Evanston's Mayor's Award, and the Medallion Award from the Children's Theatre Foundation of America.

Eric Coble's plays include *Bright Ideas, The Giver, The Velocity of Autumn*, and *My Barking Dog* and have been produced off-Broadway, around the country, and on several continents. Awards include an Emmy nomination, the AT&T OnStage Award, and the National Theatre Conference Playwriting Award. For more oddness visit www.ericcoble.com

Doug Cooney is a writer for young people in Los Angeles. His plays and musicals have been produced by the Kennedy Center, Lincoln Center Institute, the Mark Taper Forum and South Coast Repertory, among others. He is currently writing on *Sofia the First,* Disney Jr.'s new animated series for preschoolers.

Linda Daugherty received the 2011 Society for Adolescent Health and Medicine national award for her plays dealing with adolescent and teen issues. Her plays, including more lighthearted fare, more than 30 of which premiered at Dallas Children's Theater where she is playwright-in-residence, are performed worldwide. She is a member of The Dramatists Guild of America.

Lisa Dillman's award-winning plays include *Ground* (Humana Festival), *Detail of a Larger Work* (Steppenwolf Theatre Company), *Flung* and *Half of Plenty* (American Theatre Company), and *The Walls* (Rivendell Theatre Ensemble/Steppenwolf). She has been commissioned by Goodman Theatre, Steppenwolf Theatre Company, Northlight Theatre, the Chicago Humanities Festival, and Rivendell Theatre Ensemble. She lives in Chicago.

Richard Dresser's 17 published plays have been produced in New York, leading regional theaters, and in Europe. They include *Rounding Third, Below the Belt,* and a trilogy of plays about happiness in America: *Augusta, The Pursuit of Happiness,* and *A View of the Harbor.* Recent projects include the book for the musical *Johnny Baseball* and *The Hand of God* about reality television.

José Cruz González has written for Paz, the Emmy-nominated series by Discovery Kids for The Learning Channel. He was a recipient of a 2004 TCG/Pew National Theatre Residency grant. He teaches at California State University in Los Angeles and is an associate artist with Cornerstone Theater Company and playwright-in-residence with Childsplay in Phoenix.

Stephen Gregg's plays include *This Is a Test, Small Actors, S.P.A.R., Twitch, One Lane Bridge* and many others. *This Is a Test* has been on *Dramatics* magazine's list of most-produced one-acts for more than 20 years. Gregg writes the Playwright Now blog at www.schooltheatre.org.

D.W. Gregory is the author of more than half a dozen plays for young actors, including *Penny Candy* and *The Secret Lives of Toads*, also available through Dramatic Publishing.

Brian Guehring is the playwright-in-residence and education director for the Omaha Theater Company. Royalties from this play will go toward the Tracy Iwersen Pride Player Scholarship Fund for LGBT teen activists. For information about Pride Players or Brian's scripts such as *The Misfits, The Bully Show,* and *Where the Red Fern Grows,* visit his website at www.brianguehring.com

Dwayne Hartford is a playwright, director and actor originally from Maine, now living in Phoenix. He is an associate artist and playwright-in-residence with Childsplay. His play *Eric and Elliot* received the 2005 AATE Distinguished Play Award. Hartford earned his B.F.A. from the Boston Conservatory.

Barry Kornhauser: Growing up a short, freckle-faced redhead named "Kornhauser," Barry became intimately acquainted with bullying early on. He survived, however, to win the Charlotte B.Chorpenning Award, write plays for Tony Award-winning stages such as the Kennedy Center, and see his Youtheatre program honored at the White House. Happily, these days he is more intimately acquainted with his wife, Carol; children Max, Sam and Ariel; and the Fulton Theatre, where he serves as playwright-in-residence.

Trish Lindberg, Ph.D., is a professor at Plymouth State University and winner of numerous awards for her work, including the AATE National Youth Theatre Director Award. Lindberg has written and directed productions for youth and family audiences in the United States, Ireland, England, South Africa, New Zealand and Lithuania.

Brett Neveu's work includes productions with The Royal Court Theatre and Royal Shakespeare Company, as well as The House Theatre, Writers' Theatre, Goodman Theatre, and A Red Orchid Theatre, all in Chicago. He has developed work with companies including The New Group, Steppenwolf Theatre Company and Victory Gardens Theater and is an ensemble member of A Red Orchid Theatre.

Ernie Nolan is a director and playwright whose work has been featured both nationally and internationally. He is the associate artistic director of Emerald City Theatre in Chicago, the vice president of Theatre for Young Audiences USA, and teaches at The Theatre School at DePaul University.

R.N. Sandberg's plays include *A Little Princess, Anne of Green Gables, Frankenstein, Jarpteetza/The Firebird, Martina Lost and Found, The Moonstone, The Odyssey,* Bonderman winner *Can't Believe It* and *The Judgment of Bett*, developed at the Kennedy Center. His *In Between* deals with identity and bullying, and his *IRL* focuses on cyberbullying.

Geraldine Ann Snyder founded Blue Apple Players with director/husband Paul Lenzi. In addition to writing and performing in more than 40 Blue Apple Players musicals, Geraldine is an internationally known designer. Her work has been featured in *Newsweek, Craft Horizons, Decorative*

Art in Modern Interiors, *Creating Modern Furniture*, and *Contemporary Crafts of the Americas*. She is proud to have had several musicals published by Dramatic Publishing.

Werner Trieschmann's numerous plays have been produced across the United States, Canada, England and Italy. His plays, including *Failing the Improv*, *You Have to Serve Somebody* and *Disfarmer*, have been staged by Moving Arts in Los Angeles, The New Theatre in Boston, and the Arkansas Repertory Theatre. He earned an M.F.A. in playwriting from Boston University and lives in Little Rock, Arkansas.

Elizabeth Wong, playwright/director, is known for her quirky blend of social issues and comedy. Plays include *Letters to a Student Revolutionary, Dating and Mating in Modern Times, China Doll*, and *Kimchee and Chitlins*. She was a *Los Angeles Times* editorial columnist and Disney Fellow. Television credits include ABC's *All-American Girl*. www.elizabethwong.net

Y York is the proud recipient of the 2008 Smith Prize, the 2006 Hawai`i Award for Literature, a Berrilla Kerr Award, and the Charlotte B. Chorpenning Award for her body of work for children and families. York was proclaimed the 2010 Walter Wangerin Jr. fellow. She lives with Mark Lutwak and their dog friends.